MW00716152

BRINGING YOUR
'A' GAME 2.0

Inspirational Coaching to Profitability

BY CHRISTINA BLATCHFORD, DMD

AND

WILLIAM A. BLATCHFORD, DDS

Copyright © 2016
by Blatchford Solutions

All rights reserved. No part of the material protected by this copyright notice may be reproduced in whole or in part in any form without written permission from the copyright owner.

ISBN: 978-0-9823836-3-6

Book design and photo shoot concept by
Visuality
www.visuality.biz

Other books and products from Blatchford Solutions:

Playing Your 'A' Game
Dentist's Mighty Guidebook
Blatchford Blueprints
No Nonsense Transitions
The Business of Hygiene (video)
Blatchford in a Box (video)

For ordering:
888-977-4600; www.blatchford.com
P.O. Box 9070; Bend, OR 97708

Printed and bound in the United States of America
by Maverick Publications • Bend, Oregon

WE DEDICATE THIS BOOK TO

Three Precious Beings:

Luke Evans is a strong yet sensitive young man with a bright future. He is filled with kindness and clever ideas.

Grace Guthrie is studying to be an astronaut dentist. She has great enthusiasm and energy for any possibility. She is a joy with lots of laughs.

Everett Evans is independent and what a love. He likes adventure, train travel, Luke and Gracie.

PROCEEDS

While you are learning, proceeds for *Bringing Your 'A' Game 2.0* will go to Juvenile Diabetic Research Foundation (JDRF) where research is very close to encapsulation of stem cells to produce insulin for people with Type 1 Diabetes. Our goal is to have 1000 dentists donate cost from one crown for Just One Crown effort at JDRF. Every dentist knows at least one Type 1 in their patient base or in their extended family. Blatchford Solutions would like to move from Type 1 to Type NONE.

Tiffany Blatchford Evans is a Type 1, wanting to be a Type NONE as is our Blatchford consultant Nanci Granahan who became a diabetic at age 11.

CONTENTS

Introduction xi

Prologue..xviii

Warning!..xix

1   Retire As You Go 1
     — *Dr. Richard Dunn*

2   All Eyes on the Ball.................................... 9
     — *Dr. April Ziegele*

3   Moving Forward 29
     — *Dr. Tejas Patel*

4   King of Ephrata 39
     — *Dr. Brian Jacobsen*

5   Successful Merger.. 49
     — *Dr. Steve Sirin*

6   State of Grace... 57
     — *Dr. Laura Aeschlimann*

7   From the Beginning....................................... 67
     — *Drs. Tom & Tamara Fernandes & Adam Kirkpatrick*

8   Mentors 79
     — *Drs. Dennis and Marie Stiles*

9   Teeth Tomorrow 89
     — *Drs. Claudia Patch and Michael Tischler*

10   Retiring in Ten Years 101
     — *Dr. Dale Schisler*

11   The Team 109

12   A Balanced Life... 125
     — *Dr. Ben Wang*

13　Winning as a Single Mom 133
　　— *Dr. Laura Fauchier*

14　Small Town Dentist 145
　　— *Dr. Angie Cotey*

15　The Teacher 155
　　— *Dr. Kim Okamura*

16　Character Counts 165
　　— *Dr. Chris Maestro*

17　The Highly Niched Practice 173
　　— *Dr. Rhys Spoor*

18　Purchasing a Practice 189
　　— *Dr. Chris Mueller*

19　Relationship Building 205
　　— *Dr. Curtis Chan*

20　Flourishing in the Desert 221
　　— *Dr. Samir Patel*

21　Rejuvenation 231
　　— *Dr. Jeff Hadley*

22　The Breadwinning Partner 239
　　— *Dr. Tracy Davis*

23　The Gift of Giving 251
　　— *Dr. Jayson Tabor*

　　Conclusion 263

　　Additional Resources 271

ACKNOWLEDGEMENTS

We want to acknowledge all the many mentors enjoyed by the doctors in 'A' *Game*. Many of these technical mentors have taken great risks over their careers to teach and share what they know. A dental school's mandate is to have students pass the state board, nothing more, nothing less. Upon graduation, continuing education choices are made and these impact a person's life as never before.

Thank you Drs. Rosenthal, Dickerson, Kois, Nash, Spoor, Whelan, Hornbrook, Pankey, Strupp, Baird, Spear, Mopper, Farran, Trinkner, Nixon, Reed, Eubanks, Dorfman, Garg, Misch and so many more. You help doctors bring their 'A' Game and keep moving forward.

We want to thank the many people along our life's path who have made significant differences, our Blatchford Solutions team of Carol Bogner, Jeanne Swenson, Kaye Puccetti, Nanci Granahan, Keri Weron, Daniel Pite, Duke Meegan, Tiffany Evans, Nanci Huston, and Dr. Brad Bramen.

BRINGING YOUR
'A' GAME 2.0

Inspirational Coaching to Profitability

BY CHRISTINA BLATCHFORD, DMD
AND
WILLIAM A. BLATCHFORD, DDS

INTRODUCTION

Our purpose is to provide inspiration, education and motivation for dentists and teams to achieve their dream practice. The business of dentistry provides many unparalleled qualities of independence, entrepreneurial leadership, teamsmanship, total control and so many choices.

In North America, we were fortunate to be born on the right side of the planet. People do have discretionary income, their smiles and teeth are important to them and you are respected and valued as that messenger.

We enjoy the challenge of dentists who feel frustrated, unfulfilled, overworked and underpaid as well as underworked or out of control with debt and worry with business decisions. The successful business of dentistry is not complex or a secret. The real challenge is the owner and leader is also the top highly skilled mechanical operator; the only licensed diagnostician. The owner also wears a team hat and letterman's jacket. The team owner is also the head cheerleader. The dentist wears every hat and must know every position played on the team. It is easy to get lost in the crowd and not see the score board.

Herein lies the challenge and work: to help the dentist find themselves, define their standards and values, help them discover and define clearly the practice of their dreams and help them create a plan to arrive there. Using basic business principles of vision, goal setting, leadership, budgeting, communication, sales, and marketing, we coach them to achieve their dream.

I (Bill) was a practicing dentist for 20 years in Corvallis, OR. Now, our daughter Christina is a dentist who practices in Milwaukie, OR and is joining us in our dental business coaching. Our daughter, Tiffany Evans, a teacher by training, also works with us and she is able to accomplish much with two young boys.

We understand and appreciate the science and technology. We also understand the debt burden of a young dentist, business choices in partnerships and associateships, as well as the real love many dentists feel for the actual practicing along with the extraordinary generational relationships that make a practice special. Then, there is the distinct dental opportunity in continuing to practice as long as you are able and have desire. There is not another profession like it.

Dr. Bill Blatchford

After graduating from Loyola Dental School in Chicago in 1970, I (Bill) spent the next 20 years as a practicing dentist in Corvallis, Oregon. Corvallis is a college town, the home of Oregon State University. At that time, the population was 40,000 with over 50 dentists. In 1985, I was collecting more than $1.1 million. Adjusting that number for inflation and including the fact that crowns were $200, that's more than $3 million in today's dollars as a solo GP.

That's a lot of dentistry.

I've been fortunate to spend the past 26 years as a business and life coach for dentists looking to be more productive in their practices while enjoying a better work-life balance in their personal lives. I've worked with over 3,000 dentists, helping them dramatically increase their efficiency at work so they can enjoy more abundance with their families at home. Currently, Blatchford Solutions coaches approximately 50 dentists per year to enjoy a new level of success in their life and practice.

My father was a dairy farmer who 'never worked a day in his life' as he believed if we love what we do, we aren't 'working'. I learned that lesson early on as I love what I do. My high school sweetheart, Carolyn, and I have celebrated almost 50 years of married life. We have two daughters, one a dentist (following Dad's footsteps) and Blatchford Coach and the other an accomplished elementary teacher (following Mom's footsteps). Our philosophy is that life is a banquet and we participate by coaching dentists to reach their dreams, traveling the world, flying, boating, diving, skiing, hunting, fishing, cycling, and delighting in our grandchildren.

Today, our daughter Christina, a general dentist who practices in Milwaukie, Oregon, is CO-CEO of our dental business coaching, Blatchford Solutions. Our daughter, Tiffany, a teacher by training, is now working with us in marketing. Both enjoy balance in career and life with their young children, husbands, and family.

Dr. Christina Blatchford

My story in dentistry took a circuitous path. I loved French, art, drama and horses in high school. There was no room for sciences with my love of reading. I loved that my dad was so available to haul my horse around to shows and be there while I participated. I did notice my dad was more available than some fathers who had to travel but then again, it was a university town, so there never appeared to be much pressure on professors.

A university town forces public schools to be academically excellent. It also creates the athletic events, interesting speakers and opportunities for local kids to step up their game. For undergraduate studies, I wanted more than the home town college and I wanted warmth. University of Arizona was my choice for a Fashion Merchandising degree. I worked a year at Nordstrom in Horton Plaza San Diego and learned a whole degree in sales and successful conversations. I did notice all my working hours were when other young people had time off.

I decided to pursue a degree in Commercial Interior Design from Harrington Institute in Chicago, enjoying the form, function and color. I worked for six years at the largest architectural in Portland designing medical offices. With 400 architects and 60 interior designers, I could see if I became my boss, I would be working 60+ hours a week, three weeks vacation with some travel with paltry pay for the effort.

The positive was I met and married a wonderful mate. His father was an architect and he had found his profession. I did some real soul searching. What could I do that created more time, enjoyment and reward? I was searching for a brighter future and a greater lifestyle.

At age 32, I decided dentistry answered my quandary. I saw my dad had enjoyed it, had time to hunt and fish, took us nice places, did Indian Princess' with us and rode horses with me. I started taking math courses at night and quit my job to retrain. I had emotional support from my immediate family but there were doubts beyond. I chose to ignore them.

I went to Portland State for my two years of prerequisites with a number of others who were retraining. I was fortunate to be accepted at OHSU and graduated 2009. I kept asking my dad through all those science courses if this was really worth it. He told me "this is a pretty exclusive club and yes, the effort is worth it."

I was so eager to be in private practice, I actually purchased a practice in May of senior year. It originally belonged to one of the first female dentists in Oregon and for five years, was operated by a male. Many of my patients are the age of the original dentist and have great stories.

Because the dental school is in Portland, there is a real saturation of dentists. The ratio is currently 500 people per dentist. For that reason, I chose to practice on the East side, a more blue-collar area.

Even though I chose dentistry as a third career, I was drawn to organization and efficiency. I make decisions easily and dislike planning meetings. I have learned from each team member and keep working towards my best. I love the business and leadership part of dentistry.

Initially, I felt I had little efficiency. My dad showed me the 90 second crown prep and to schedule an hour. Wow! All kinds of little things can make an office more efficient and in this digital age, there shouldn't be any misplaced papers.

Dad encouraged me to work three days and be completely off for four days. We have a six-year-old enthusiastic daughter who approaches everything with joy. Those are precious times which can never be replaced. Thus, I start a Monday with a grin. I am rested and ready.

Now, my dad and I work together on the Business of Dentistry. I had no idea I would become so energized by coaching other doctors. We receive emails from Asia and Latin America asking how to be successful. Here is some business advice for the new dentist:

- Decide who you are, and what kind of practice you ultimately desire.

- Do your demographics to find the desirable location and gamble it will be solid for next thirty years

- Ideal: Find a practice to purchase in that area.

- Make sure you have your own representative looking out for you, your interests and your money. Do not believe the selling broker is your friend.

- Ask for tax returns, profit and loss, fee schedules, insurance collections, debt structure and staffing. Red flag—"I can't find it, you don't need to see all that," says the seller.

- Create a contract that the selling doctor must depart immediately. There is no "indefinite departure" as selling doctor will work on "his" patients. How can they be "his" patients when he just sold you the practice?

- Step up and be the boss, not just the person paying the bills. Staff is loyal to the selling doctor and you will need to work well at shifting their trust and loyalty.

- Make only positive statements about the selling doctor. You were not there when the work was placed. These patients are loyal to the departing doctor. You cannot buy their loyalty. Work at it.

- Do not make a long-term treatment plan at the first hygiene visit. Let patients become acquainted with you and approach them on the second visit.

Many times with young dentists, I see difficult situations after the fact. Currently, a popular method is for a doctor to have a younger partner buy in for 49%, the selling doctor retaining 51% control. Buyer beware: Just because someone has been in practice for twenty years does not mean there is money to split the net in half. The assumption is

One Plus One equals Three which means not only did you purchase a minority share, you also now must create new patients and build your practice. In some instances, the new doctor does not see any hygiene patients for treatment. By the selling doctor retaining 51%, he is still the leader in the eyes of the staff and the 49% doctor is the "interloper." This is a challenging situation when one doctor is unhappy.

There is joy however, in Mudville when a doctor again becomes excited about dentistry and does not want to quit. When we are able to help create a "Retire As You Go" scenario with team and patients while the doctor continues for as long as he is able or desires; this is very rewarding.

Buy this book for your peers, your specialists, your children and grandchildren. Inspire others to be part of this unique and very special profession.

Christina Blatchford

*Daughter, Gracie, wins
1st place in Lead Line*

PROLOGUE

Dentistry can be so rewarding emotionally and financially if done well. Certain practices are very successful. They know themselves very well, they have standards and are able to communicate those values with passion and energy.

One thing is very clear, even with dentists—that behavior with its impending results, is a choice. We are at choice every minute of the day. What we choose to do with the paths presented us, is a choice. In dentistry, putting up with unskilled average staff is a choice, not being accountable for your own actions is a choice, having an overhead of 83% is a choice, selecting a poor quality laboratory is a choice, avoiding "expensive" continuing education courses is a choice, being frustrated in dentistry is a choice, trying to copy others instead of discovering yourself is a choice.

The good news is you can change your behavior. You can change your choice.

WARNING!

These doctors have shared their stories, ideas, worries and goals to help you. Their practices are unique due to their training, personality, vision, location, experience and marketing. There is only one April Ziegele, Brian Jacobsen or Adam Kirkpatrick. You can use their ideas and it will be unique in your practice, but not exactly like theirs.

They have full time practices, just as you. Please respect this. We purposely did not list contact numbers. PLEASE DO NOT CALL THESE DOCTORS!

If you have a question, please contact them through their websites. They may return your email inquiry.

Another avenue for information is to contact us at www.blatchford. com or Jeanne Swenson in our Bend office at 541-389-9088.

1

RETIRE AS YOU GO

Dr. Richard Dunn

When Dr. Dunn came to Blatchford at age 58, he was disillusioned about dentistry, and with a staff of 17, owned a management nightmare. He even suggested a new path—an internet marketing venture with his son would be his future. He thought of giving up dentistry. He was ready to retire before he met Dr. Blatchford.

Now, he has a team of five, he feels stronger as a leader. He feels empowered. Now, he does dentistry and comes home, a positive separation. He has set a new tone for patient care and fun. "The team is more productive than ever," Dr. Dunn proudly proclaims.

He makes strong points about Blatchford coaching:

- Falling in love again with dentistry and no longer stressed

- Finding the reason for being a dentist

- Became a better dentist by being more relaxed and focused.

- Being around so many outstanding clinicians and Blatchford coaches have been a positive force that encourages us to strive to always be better to ascend to the top of our profession

- Became a much better leader and manager of my dental practice.

I see items that need to be addressed and now I DO THEM—I do no procrastinate.

- I lead by example for my team and have established positive atmosphere at the office

- Team is encouraged to improve themselves through education and use their creativity to not only improve our office and patient care but also be part of the 'fixing issues" at the office.

- Increased time off from the practice is huge. Planning and taking trips to places I never thought I would get to, spending lots of time with my wife, my sons and family is PRICELESS.

- Life is GREAT. I am reinvigorated.

Dr. Dunn practices in Elmira, NY, population 35K with 30 dentists. One of several things that brand his practice is the treatment of sleep apnea. He had been interested in sleep medicine as he is also a patient. When he started with Blatchford Coaching, sleep medicine bloomed for him as he met Dr. Steven Greenman, a Blatchford associate who has an on-line course sharing medical billing, advertising and making it all work. (drscg1@gmail.com)

Dr. Dunn has become a Diplomat of the American Board of Dental Sleep Medicine. There are about 270 Diplomates and it takes 2 to 2.5 years to obtain these credentials. What it has done for Dr. Dunn is increased his enthusiasm, interest and expertise in sleep medicine and created a mutual respect and credibility to discuss sleep medicine with all branches of medicine. Dr. Dunn is now an equal to physicians in his knowledge and interest. He is receiving the majority of his referrals for sleep medicine from physicians in the area, especially from two different pulmonary groups in Elmira.

He also uses radio ads plus referrals from internal marketing as well as Heath Fairs. He has four sleep testing devices for patients to take home with ability for a sleep physician to monitor the results. Dr. Dunn has done Lunch and Learns in specialty practices and now his team effectively does Lunch and Learns with other team members. He has also spoken to Board Certified sleep physicians and a group of general dentists in the area refer to Dr. Dunn.

He admits it is a slow process to gain credibility. One has to expand referring circles. He now has a physical therapist who does TMJ work and is now referring to Dr. Dunn for sleep apnea.

His goal is 20 sleep cases a month. For Dr. Dunn, sleep apnea has a $3200 case value and team completes 95% of the work. He works on acknowledging referrals and constant communication is key, especially with physicians.

Dr. Dunn feels he is branded by how he and his team treat patients. They work on their phone skills. Dr. calls patients at night and the night before a new patient comes in, Dr. Dunn calls to see if they might have some questions. The result is a quicker bond before they have ever met Dr. Dunn. The conversations start quickly.

A merger was a positive result for Dr. Dunn. He did not buy equipment and he did not criticize the selling doctor's work. Bill coached Dr. Dunn to offer a flat fee per chart when patients came into his office. The selling doctor had three failed attempts at selling his practice so there were not a ton of patients but nearly 400 great patients with tremendous dental needs arrived at Dr. Dunn's door. Bill coached him to go slow with conversations about treatment. Instead, make a friend by evaluating patients and prioritizing treatment. The merging practice was on the opposite side of town, about 25-mile drive for many of the patients. Most patients said to Dr. Dunn, "I knew all along that he wanted to retire but was comfortable with the doctor."

Dr. Dunn's second favorite treatment is restoring implants. He does not do the surgery as he works closely with great oral surgeons in town. He has toyed with doing implant training but it works so well right now, he has not taken that step.

His office goal is $12K a day working a 3½ days a week with nine weeks of vacation. Bonus? His staff has never missed a BAM bonus since he has been with Blatchford and averages $1000+ per month with highs of $3000+.

Dr. Dunn and his wife, Nancy, an accomplished cellular biologist, have raised two adult boys. One was aiming at a pro-baseball career when an injury sidelined that and he is now with a restaurant in Deer Valley, UT and another son is a financial advisor in Rochester. Dr. Dunn is so pleased with the changes in his practice, he sees more years of profitability and pleasure. He sees quite a number of older dentists in Elmira and more mergers in the curtains.

rdunn@stny.rr.com

Playing the Blatchford Game: Retire As You Go

Dr. Richard Dunn has taken the concept of Retire As You Go and made a life skill out of it. He is in love with dentistry, excited about the new changes, takes excellent continuing education and can see he could continue to practice into his seventies. One of the main advantages is you can create this in any fashion you desire. You can take every other month off and work 15 days in between. Find a staff who sees the same thing and continue the income stream as well as the emotional joy of feeling needed.

Many important factors are creating an opportunity for dentists to practice their skills years beyond the normal retirement age. Because of changes in our demographics, economics, longevity and a renewed passion for dentistry, we have reached a new career opportunity in what we call the "Retire As You Go" program.

The factors making "Retire As You Go" a real force are:

Dental boomers are reaching retirement age at about 6,800 a year and dental schools are currently graduating 4,000 a year. Consequently, the dream of selling your practice for a bundle is fading fast. The formula for sale has been 1.5 times net. Keep practicing for 18 more months and throw the key in the river on the way home! You would be even, if you could sell.

Females comprise about 40% of graduating classes and statistically, are practicing 12 years. Many are associating so as to raise a family. A new dentist is likely married to a professional whose employment may be limited in your town. Consequently, dental graduates are forced to be more selective in location than 40 years ago.

Many dentists were depending on the stock market boom to retire early. For many, the retirement nest egg has a big crack.

We are living longer. How old are your parents? The self-employed American male dies within 18 months of retirement. Why? Because the status and structure of what has been the norm is gone.

It takes emotional and spiritual skills to retire well, psychologically. Why retire at 55 and become depressed?

Newer technologies in all phases of dentistry allow the passion to return within the profession. Sixty-five-year-old dentists are saying, "I wish we had these materials 30 years ago and that I was 30 years younger. This is great fun."

The paradigm can shift as to what constitutes a dental practice, when you work, who will work with you and what treatments you will render.

Every person's retirement dream is different. As with dentists, there is no set box you must fit. The true "Retire As You Go" program is filled with personal choice. As you reach middle age, you have earned a reputation of excellence and probably been a standard in a community for 25 years. Keep the same patient base who generally match your age.

If you continue practicing in some fashion, you need to revisit the vision of yourself and change your paradigm of practice. "Retire As You Go" means your days of practicing full out four days a week, ten-hour days are over. Our longevity is not ours to choose, however, you can still make some smart choices and plans.

Ask yourself, for the future, three questions—Who am I, What do I do, For Whom do I do it? Then think long and hard about what patients you have enjoyed the most, what treatments still offer intrigue and what treatments you would most like to eliminate. Think of the offerings outside of dentistry and build your dental life around those. Would you like to take a month off at a time, would you practice three days a week with a week off every month? The choices are yours. If you are clear about your practice plans and have enthusiasm and direction, you will find teams who want what you want.

Your speaking to staff and patients is positive.... "I am so in love with dentistry; the thought of fully retiring is appalling. What I am doing instead is staying in the field and continuing to be technically competent. Instead of rushing here and there to take continuing education, I will take a week to enjoy the museums, golf and dining."

You must continue to show enthusiasm and amazement with dentistry. You can create this any way you want. For it to be successful, you must communicate your love of dentistry rather than wanting to escape from it. Dr. Omer Reed is an excellent model. A curious bright man, he practiced nine 10-day cycles annually. He and his wife attended continuing education and took notes like they were hearing it for the first time. Would Omer ever retire? I doubt it and you, too, can create your own "Retire As You Go" in dentistry.

Bill Blatchford, DDS

From the Blatchford Playbook:
Loyalty to Local Team

- ▶ Support the home town businesses and teams

- ▶ Buy your cars locally

- ▶ Gift baskets should include local products

- ▶ Support local faires and events with your signature food booth and give money to charity

- ▶ Know your local industries so you can ASK intelligent questions, i.e. "How's the soybean harvest?" "I hear you won a contract," etc.

- ▶ Buy products locally even if it costs a little more

- ▶ We are global. Think how that product will help a local businessperson (that is what you are, too)

- ▶ Select Christmas gifts from local industries

- ▶ Be a "cheerleader" for your town, community. Attend concerts, sports events, openings, Chamber of Commerce Field Days, fundraisers, potlucks, high school art shows, etc.

- ▶ Arrange for a local high school scholarship for entry in the dental industry: assistant, lab tech, hygiene or pre-dent.

2

ALL EYES ON THE BALL

Dr. April Ziegele

A successful balance was April Ziegele's desire when she began working with us. How to juggle a large fast-paced practice in a small Washington town, keep being a great wife and friend to her husband, be an integral and influential part of raising two toddlers, be a grateful daughter and spiritually active?

A graduate of Loma Linda, April wanted to associate for five years and then make some choices. In her first associateship, Dr. Ziegele saw beautiful dentistry being delivered in twelve-hour days with everyone running ragged. She knew she was not giving her best and was very frustrated. She knew in her heart she had different goals of how guests should be treated and dentistry delivered.

After six weeks, the owner took her to lunch and offered her the practice. Yikes! April was just out of school and naïve enough to think $890K was the norm. Yet, she realized her payments would be $14K a month and she would be responsible for all bills, including staff. She had no idea how to make a practice operate with two full time doctors and staff of fourteen.

"I was so afraid that I would end up bankrupt and my family would suffer for ten years. I lost so much sleep, my husband Jon was afraid for me and shared that he thought we should not proceed with the sale. I asked my professors from dental school and one said 'run for the hills' and the other said 'go for it.'" A small, rural lumber mill town, Sumner (pop. 8,504 in 2000) is 35 miles south of Seattle and had tulip and daffodil farms. By a stroke of luck, in 2001, Sumner became the starting terminal for the Seattle commuter train. Sumner is now growing at 6% a year.

Yet, in 1997, four months out of dental school, running a huge practice with no leadership experience was agonizing. A big case was four crowns at a time. A/R reached $220K. In 1998, they sent 489 statements monthly which took three days to process. The computers crashed and they discovered the backup had never worked.

Dr. Ziegele went through four associate doctors in four years. Each seemed to want to work for a year and run the practice how they wanted when April was not present. April made a real point to honor and compliment her staff but it seemed they, too, took more and more each day. Embarrassed to admit it, at one point she said to her staff, "Why don't you all just suck my blood out too, and get it over with?" She wondered why she didn't go into hygiene.

Dr. Ziegele took three weeks off to have Christopher in March of 1999. She was working 12-hour days and had an overhead of 78%. Patients and colleagues criticized her but the pressure was there. Her second child was born in 2001 when the associate was not a great producer. "He was content to do just the bare minimum and would send his patients home instead of doing the work." April was so frustrated as she was leaving for work before the babies were awake and arriving home when they were down for the night.

When April met Lori Huber, a Blatchford enrollment coach, April shared she wanted to spend more time with her two babies. It was a very emotional meeting and a turning point for her to enjoy dentistry, become more profitable and be a mother again.

Starting Blatchford coaching, Dr. Ziegele was producing $1M a year with a 73% overhead. She had two doctors, two hygienists and a staff of 14. A/R was $195K and each of the 50 new patients a month were told they needed to first have a full new patient exam with the doctor and they could eventually get their teeth cleaned. They were working 69 hours a week with one week vacation.

Now, they are attracting 30 new patients a month, work 22 hours a week and take nine weeks time off with pay, have one doctor, two hygienists and a team of two dental assistants and one receptionist with overhead at 48% and produce $1.8M.

Previously, April felt she selected her staff poorly and lacked leadership skills. As a new graduate, Dr. Ziegele was looking for skilled staff rather than attitude. This was especially true in hiring associates. April left leadership up to her "office manager" and then yelled at her when she didn't get "it" right (she deeply regrets those times). She was so busy in the trenches trying to find her way out; she had no vision that was clearly stated. Everyone just did the best they could and "obviously, this did not work."

April would go to a class and come home with great ideas. Monday morning she would tell her staff, "This is what we are going to do—do it now." They knew she didn't really mean it, plus, they had no idea how to implement. "Often I would let staff say whatever and I would just avoid confrontation instead of handling an issue. This just made things worse."

Dr. Ziegele always felt she would be successful. Selecting dentistry in the medical field, she figured it would be a good income while being a mother, too. Her childhood dentist reminded her recently that at seven years of age, April said she was going to be a dentist and she never wavered from that goal. However, once she purchased this large practice, she knew she was in over her head. "I recently ran into a sales rep in our area who told me she could just look at me then and know I was just keeping my head above water."

Though her family moved all over, they always considered Seattle home. When April graduated, she and Jon looked for a "cosmetic practice" and found a great match as the dentist was AACD accredited.

In her transition from ragged to wonderful, she took the time to clearly write and express her vision. Her picture for her practice was always there but daily she was so busy staying afloat she never communicated it to the busy staff. Once the direction was clear of who they are and what they do, systems were put in place to create the results of which April dreamed.

Block booking was mandatory. A daily goal and bonus system were critical. Learning sales skills and offering comprehensive care was essential. Firm financial arrangements were made as well as clear com¬munications of meaningful morning meetings, evening meetings to end the day, weekly staff meetings, and monthly training sessions called BMW 4x4 (Blatchford Motivational Workshop held for four hours every four weeks). These meetings have since progressed to BMW 2x2 two-hour meetings, since their team has been together for 14+ years! Guest protocol systems were introduced as well as marketing. April stopped doing the treatments she disliked—extractions, and implants. Crabbiness ended.

Simultaneously, April stepped up her leadership skills. When she made the decision to be coached by Blatchford, one of her fourteen staff said, "We can do this ourselves. I don't think we need Dr. Blatchford." April's new leadership response was, "I have already decided the path we are taking. Your choice is whether you want to work here or not."

"I think it is really tough to be a woman in a leadership position. I struggle with it all the time. I want to be friends (April is a very high I on DISC test) with my team, hang out with them, etc., like they do with each other. I can, to some extent, but not completely since I have chosen to be the leader. This is hard for me. It is a very fine line. I really struggle with decisions that impact the staff—especially cutting positions. I am getting better and I have learned that once I am frustrated enough to think about letting someone go, I have already gone about eight months further than I should have."

"And I have a fabulous team who encourage me on a daily basis. For example, recently Jon and I purchased a new home. Five years ago, the staff comments would be, "It must be nice to have all that money to do that kind of thing." Now I hear, "Good for you, we're proud of you to make the decision, we can hardly wait to see it, how can we help?" What a difference! I know the biggest difference was just deciding to be the leader instead of waiting to see if someone else would just do it. You should hear me on the way to work. I listen to Brian Tracy's Maximum Achievement. At the stoplight, I turn it off and say out loud, 'I am going to lead with compassion and empathy. I will make my team and guests feel good about themselves today and I will have a blast doing it.' I have to do this every single day. I have to."

Dr. Ziegele does not consider herself a natural leader. She does possess an extraordinary amount of enthusiasm, passion and conviction as well as a killer sense of humor about the world and herself. Her excitement is contagious. "Once I told them exactly what I wanted, we talked about it every single day at first, then every single week for a while and now once a month—they caught the vision. Now they are pushing all of us to improve. Other leadership skills she has learned:

Dealing with small things immediately, no festering of non communicated items. April makes the final decision after asking her team's input. This is not a democracy. Communicate appreciation and celebrate their milestones. Each staff member carries April's vision as if it were their own.

She sees leadership as being the torch bearer for encouragement and optimism. "I cannot have my team see me freaking out," April confides. Some days when the morning blocks are not full, the team takes it personally. Instead of freaking out over an unfilled schedule, they practice their sales skills, transfers and role playing to increase "quality case acceptance."

Another area of leadership April struggles with is eliminating staff positions. Moving the team from fourteen to five was really difficult because she liked them all. "When I couldn't figure out what they were doing, I knew I HAD to do something." Since the Ziegele team is composed of six, including the doctor, everyone is completely cross-trained. All can excellently answer the phone, change appointments, make financial arrangements, consult or do initial conversations, clean or setup a room and run instruments. "We will NEVER interrupt a member who is with a guest." April feels it is critical for doctors to do whatever it takes to get the job done. Because they are cross trained, they all see the opportunity and do not have to be asked.

The hardest decision she had to make was to cut hours from 69 a week to 22. "I will tell you that it almost took medical intervention for me to drop that last ½ day and truly go to only 3 days/week. My team looked to me to be the leader, and kept telling me that we could do it, but I still had all the bills to pay. Of course they wanted to do it, they would still get paid for the full 28 hours!! But I made the decision, and I've never looked back or regretted it. Our production just went up, and I was able to spend the time with my family that I craved."

What has the Ziegele practice done to brand themselves, to make them stand apart?

Being an all women team, they genuinely enjoy each other. They think about the creature comforts which might be overlooked. For example, their post-op bags are stocked with items they would love to receive. Their environment reflects women and they have great empathy when women say, "I don't want to look older."

Choosing to be excellent is everything they do. They do not compromise—ever. They are not trying to be everyone's dentist, just those in search of the very best.

Putting their families first, Dr. Ziegele has a family photo in the entryway to tell everyone right away what is Priority Number One. The Ziegele team puts their family first, too.

April feels her team of five is extremely motivated by several things: the bonus system is a monetary reward for being focused, skilled and going beyond ordinary. The team loves playing the game and checking daily to see how they are doing. Secondly, is the fact that April adores them and trusts them implicitly. "I talk about how great they are in front of them, each other and our guests. Wherever I go, I tell people how awesome my team is!"

When the Ziegele team is playing their 'A' game, there is no stopping them. "The energy is so contagious, it seems we can do no wrong. Treatment is accepted, we are having fun, it is almost like being 'high' on drugs, except we are simply high on life. We seem to gain energy as we go, no fatigue at the end of the day—we can hardly wait to get going again. The feeling seems to spread as our guests feel it, talk about it and even the mailman mentioned it."

April says, "My team rocks! They are simply amazing—they sell dentistry, make guests feel good, enjoy each other, lift each other up, laughing and smiling. I feel so blessed to have them enjoy this journey with me and I let them know that. I can't wait to write $6,000 bonus checks and hope to be writing $10K bonus checks each. The enthusiasm it generates just sells more dentistry. What an amazing gift to be working with such professionals on a daily basis."

Average bonus currently is $3100 monthly each. Goal is to double in next 12 months which means two more smiles per bonus time and equals talking with about ten guests of their dream smile. Team (April does not call them staff, as that is an infection!) is actively looking for the opportunity. "There is no more complaining, whining, or gossiping because we don't have time anymore. We now have a credit balance because the team recognizes that is their money. They have bought into the "ownership" of the practice due to bonuses and it makes my job so much easier."

Originally, April hated dentures. However, she is coachable and now has a cosmetic denture for $7000. She is learning to love them, do well with them and enjoy the response from guests.

Gathering 30 quality and curious new patients a month is done through marketing plans both internal and external. "We try to make our office as pleasant as possible." With a complete dental spa, they communicate their appreciation and ask for referrals. They communicate with email messages and updates (this is Seattle, remember). They give out ice cream, frappuccinos and cookies to every guest. April has created a drawer full of Starbucks cards, movie certificates, and stickers, and encourages staff to give them to guests. "We treat them so well, they rave about us wherever they go."

April has found great success with her website www.aprilziegele. com She has three search engines hosting her website and the response in computer savvy Seattle area is most worthwhile. She posted a "temporary banner" on the roof of her practice, "Accepting new patients—www.aprilziegele.com."

Externally, Dr. Ziegele focused on a mailer and it worked because Sumner is growing rapidly. The team realized this golden growth opportunity to meet new people and joined the networking groups of Chamber of Commerce, Lion's Club and Rotary. Every six months, they walk downtown on an afternoon to distribute information about their office, greet people, invite them for a tour and complimentary spa service. They dine in a different local restaurant once a week, in their uniforms and receive much attention. They have also networked with the largest bulb farm in the area to participate and advertise at all their events.

Beyond that, April has budgeted big marketing dollars and a long range plan with Tyson Steele of Eugene, OR. Results are happening.

Being ready for anything, recently the Ziegele group was on Bravo for Show Dogs Mom and Dads and the blurb was picked up by Access Hollywood and Extra. Sumner locals called April's office saying they had seen them on television.

April feels she is profitable because her vision is so clear and she never wavers from it. She has written goals, and a team and family to keep her accountable. "I am enthusiastic about my vision and can hardly wait to move forward. Team and guests are drawn to a winning combination."

April is a real fan of Dr. Rhys Spoor and has taken his anterior, posterior and occlusion courses. She has passed the written exam and taken the courses for AACD accreditation. She has a goal to produce and collect $2M by 2017 as well as reaching insurance freedom in 2018. 40% of her collections are from insurance and Delta is half of that. In Washington, that is Microsoft, Boeing and school districts. The Ziegele team is mentally free of insurance as they realize "insurance does not believe in the dentistry we believe in." They have added Illumisure, an in-office "loyalty club" for those that have no insurance, so that they can also receive the benefits of having insurance, and it is working well.

April started this journey when Christopher was only 2½ years old, and Lauren was 6 months old. She felt as though she was missing out on so much of their lives. Christopher is now 17, and a senior in high school while Lauren is 15 and a sophomore. She no longer feels like she misses out on family time. In fact, she's almost always home before her kids are now, and is ALWAYS able to be at their events at school. Christopher is the ASB President this year, and she loves that she can help him out with everything that he is doing. Both kids are in the touring choir and the touring bell choir, and she can help with both of those as well—things she says that she wouldn't have been able to do before hiring Blatchford. While still busy, she is always happy to talk to another dentist about the Blatchford program, because, as she says, "It completely changed my life!"

"Along this journey, there have many ups and downs. But I've always had the support and encouragement of not only Bill and Christina, but also all of the other Blatchford docs—I cannot tell you how nice that is! We're all in the trenches 'together', so to speak. In this dental world, where so many dentists are eager to toss each other to the wolves, it's just so nice to have a group that encourages each other, lifts each other up, shares both the wins and the losses with each other. You can learn from those that have 'been there, done that', and from those that are still trying to find their footing. I mean, really, where else can you ask a question about a difficult case, and get an answer from six dentists, not to mention RHYS SPOOR?!?! Yes, I love that. I love the support. I love the camaraderie. I love my career, and I'm not at all sure that I still would love it if things had not changed in a radical way 14 years ago. So, yes, the very best decision I have ever made was to hire Bill Blatchford. You may think I am just saying this because this is their book but I absolutely believe it to be true. I would still be wandering about—doing one crown at a time, fighting with staff to appreciate each other and me, still talking about all the things we're doing wrong at staff meetings. Instead, I LOVE what I'm doing, surrounded by a team who loves it, each other and all of our guests. My only wish is that I had made the Blatchford decision earlier. It was a bargain at five times the cost. Once he helped me establish the blocks which were keeping me from getting what I wanted, I went forward one at a time. This is fun stuff!

"I am still challenged by home and work life. I refuse to take one into the other. It really doesn't matter to my team or guests if I was up all night with a sick kid, or my husband left my car on empty or the cat threw up on the carpet. And my family doesn't want to hear about a whining guest we had today. They all deserve my undivided attention. In the back of my mind is always my family and my practice—it's what I decide to focus on that makes the difference.

"I heard once in a movie someone complaining that something was too hard. The response (I will never forget) 'Of course, it's hard. If it wasn't hard, everyone would be doing it.' That is the way I look at it. I don't want to be like everyone else. I want to be extraordinary and have an exceptional life. So yeah, it's going to be hard. Bring it on!"

www.aprilziegele.com

Playing the Blatchford Game: Take Action To Sell

Dr. Ziegele was greatly inspired by hands-on participation in two of Dr. Rhys Spoor's cosmetic courses. April and her team could see the possibilities of becoming accomplished in cosmetics along with a steady general dentistry practice. Hands on cosmetic courses mix well with the Blatchford skills in non-pressure patient driven case presentation. Dr. Ziegele's team is mastering these skills and their numbers demonstrate their commitment.

The motivation and excitement generated when a dentist learns modern ideal dentistry is the new high point in her dental life. The enthusiasm a "born-again" dentist exhibits is undeniably contagious. We have seen dentists, looking forward to retirement, take a live patient course, and now become so excited about practicing dentistry again that they develop a "retire-as-you-go" program. Taking a live patient course is a real renewal.

A gap occurs when the newly regenerated dentist returns to practice and finds for some reason, the patients are not eager to have the modern, ideal dentistry. Patients seem to respond with, "But do I need this?" "Will my insurance cover this?" "I don't really want to change things, I just want my teeth to look just like they do now." The dentist gets stuck, reverts back to education and pictures on the bracket table.

The patient's answer will probably be a stall, "I'd like to think about it," or "I'm not interested in cosmetics."

The gap occurs because we try to use the old, heavy pressure system of presentation, learned when needed dentistry was the answer to crisis-care. Dentists are slow to accept the paradigm that dentistry is optional, elective care. Patients know they do not need what we have to offer. Therefore, the old pressure system of technical education and "you really need to have this done" mentality needs to change. Because modern dentistry is a choice, an option, the sales approach needs to be one of creating dreams and offering choices. Education and technical drawings are not a part of the emotional sales process. Because the old sales approach of technical education is used to present the new modern, ideal dentistry, patients are not wildly accepting of a new smile. What is needed here is a new action to accompany your new modern skills. Successful dental sales have moved into the ethical and emotional arena, leaving the technical area behind. The action necessary is advancing your skills in sales.

Frustration can occur when a dentist learns the modern dentistry and perceives he cannot sell this beautiful dentistry "on my patients, in my town, in this blue-collar area, in this heavy insurance town, in this college town," etc. Our own paradigms of years in traditional dentistry hold us down. Change comes slowly in dentistry.

Do you have modern dentistry in your own mouth to match what you are offering your patients? Does your staff believe in and have smiles, which match what you have to offer? Patients will wonder why you are offering them beautiful optional smiles when it is very apparent you do not believe in it yourself. Walk your talk.

Part of the action we need to take is a delving into our own mental psychology. We hold ourselves down with our own self-imposed lids to greatness. Fine dentistry will have a better chance of acceptance in your practice if you believe your patients deserve to know about these choices, that you are the dentist who has the technical skills to deliver, that it is all right for you to charge a fair fee. Another part of the mental game is for thirty years, we have allowed insurance companies to dictate our treatment, our fees and our return. Dentists have also allowed the insurance companies to do our marketing and sales. Insurance companies brought in new patients and patients learned about insurance maximums, accepting treatment to that limit. If you are fearful of breaking through the insurance barrier, not only is this a mental question but also, specific skills and financial considerations are essential to have in order before becoming a non-provider.

It is exciting to coach a doctor who is taking technical classes in bonded dentistry to shift the paradigm from needed to optional and teaching scripts, which have the patient driving the conversation. We coach our doctors to concurrently take action in the live-patient process of learning. We can teach you how to sell the treatment of dreams. You must also be able to technically deliver what you can now sell.

The action is concurrent: technical and the skill of selling dreams.

Bill Blatchford, DDS

From the Blatchford Play Book: Choosing the Team

Dr. Ziegele's team is the envy of many. She and her team of five have bought into the practice vision and are the messengers of that dream. Whittling the team from a high of 14, these people have selected each other.

► We want to fly with the eagles, no turkeys allowed

► Select on a winning attitude, skills can be learned

► If a team member says, "I don't do…," they cannot be on this team

► Hire curious people who want to win

► If the applicant asks about benefits early, it is a clue

► Hire givers, not takers

► In trying out for the team, offer an applicant a "working interview."

► Set high standards for yourself and your team. Hire to those standards

► Hire for a specific position

► Hire people persons, look for healthy relationships in their lives

► Acting together as a group, you can accomplish things no individual acting alone could ever hope to bring about

► Great plays happen when unselfish and disciplined individuals are more concerned with end results than with personal ones.

► The better the team plays, the better you play

► Great teams do not do it for individual glory. They do it because they love one another

► It's amazing how much you can accomplish if no one cares who gets the credit

► Know that behavior is always a choice

My Vision

Atmosphere:

- Contagious enthusiasm and energy, individual time and attention for guests one at a time

- Each guest receives extra special attention, from the minute they walk in the door to when they leave - there is no question that this is a special experience that they will remember and rave about.

- We include coffee mugs, juice, water, warm blankets, massage pads on chairs, paraffin dips, and bags for our guests after long procedures which include Advil packets, water bottle, tissue packet with office logo on them, lip gloss, and mints.

- There is no yelling in the hallways.

- When somebody needs something, they simply get up and get it.

- Our studios are completely ready prior to bringing guests back.

- We work from a checklist to make sure we are prepared.

- BUSINESS TEAM - staff wearing uniforms. Look professional, clean, pressed -no bare legs or sandals. They are friendly to every single person, have time to chat with our guests, go over all financial options with each guest so that each one feels they can afford the very best dental treatment. They answer the phone with a smile in their tone, using our script.

- CLINICAL TEAM - staff wear nice clothing, such as: Black dress pants with dark blue blouses. They have on white lab jackets. They are not stressed, but instead are relaxed with our guests, know that there is plenty of time to make them feel comfortable. We remember the important details of their lives. We offer each guest a blanket, massage pad, paraffin wax prior to treatment. We also have small gifts for our guests that we offer with their treatment. We let our best guests know that we appreciate them and request a referral.

- This is a group that enjoys each other. They are constantly "talking up" each other, including me. We spend time letting each other know that we feel they are important. There is no bickering. There is no complaining. There is no whining.

Dental Treatment

- We are all up to date on the very best dentistry available. We let our guests know what's possible. We never offer less than the best because we believe our guests cannot afford it. Instead, we offer financial arrangements to make it comfortable for them.

- I know that my skill levels are superior because of the CE I have taken, and my staff knows this as well. They feel very comfortable recommending treatment to our guests. I will have the very best clinical and technical skills available and will actively seek out CE to improve even further. I will take one LVI, John Kois, or Rhys Spoor course each year.

- We spend quality time with each guest and they understand what we are recommending and how it will improve their smile. Our guests feel that we take time with them, they know that we care. We are known in town as the place to go for excellence.

- We work with a lab that cares as much as we do. The shades are right on the first try, and our guests are thrilled with their new smiles instead of aggravated that they have come back so many times.

- We will treat mainly adults, very few children, and will only treat the children that are well behaved. All others we will refer out to a specialist.

- We will stop advertising for all new patients and be more selective. We will become a word of mouth referral office.

Miscellaneous

- We work three days each week. Our schedule is easy to do, and everyone enjoys coming to work.

- The team feels they are well compensated and that motivates them to do even more. I want each member of our team to be compensated at no less than $50,000 per year. I want our team to be the best paid in our area and the best trained.

- We will be insurance independent by July 4.

- We will produce and collect a minimum of two million dollars, which will give each team member a bonus of $43,000 each year.

- Our team enjoys their job. They feel they have more responsibility, more control over their career direction. They are happy and enthusiastic because their environment is pleasant and low stress.

- The team all pulls together to make the office a success. The more successful the office is, the more successful each team member. We share our profitability.

- Our team enjoys fabulous vacations and time off with family. They are not worn out from working, but energized and ready to go at it again. We will take one week paid time off after every six weeks working.

- I enjoy coming to work because the stress level is lower. I know that we will meet our goals, and that we will collect the money from our guests.

- We will stop depending on insurance and instead concentrate on what is the best for our guests and what THEY want. We will give our guests what they want. We will never again say, "If we wait six months you'll have new insurance benefits."

- We will all enjoy our time off from the office. We will have the best-treated staff in our entire area, and they will brag about this at dental conventions.

- We will all attend CE and be excited about starting the new things we have learned about. Once each year we will attend the AACD convention as a team, traveling to fun and exciting locations together. We will bring the enthusiasm and team spirit back to the office.

- We will all handle problems in the same systematic approach. We will be scripted and consistent. In spite of this, each person will know that they can do the job the best way that THEY can within the set parameters.

- There will be no associate doctor.

- We will no longer serve the guests that drive us all crazy. When we find that we have a person like this in our office we will take steps immediately to eliminate this problem. We will not "feel bad" for the people that are high stress for us. We will do what works to make us all happy and productive, including removing some guests from our office active files.

Lifestyle

- Our team will enjoy their time off and be rejuvenated for the work ahead.

- Our team will have the finances available to do what they want to do and will have fun doing it.

3

MOVING FORWARD

Dr. Tejas Patel

Tejas Patel is a very happy camper near Austin, TX. He is a bright boy and an excellent leader who sees a bigger picture for himself, family and contributions beyond to help mankind.

He is from very supportive families on both sides. He and his wife, Ami, a specialist in oil and gas acquisitions, are raising two girls, ages 10 and 12. From Blatchford Coaching, Tejas was seeking a balanced lifestyle and a larger net.

He now works 190 days a year with eight weeks off. He has breakfast and dinner at home with his family, takes his girls to school three times a week and they have noted, he has Fridays and weekends off.

At Tejas' Summit with Blatchford, he learned that life and family come first and he can build a practice to support that lifestyle rather than having the practice run him with his family getting what is left. Tejas shared that with family and his extended family, now, all the Patels are really forward focused on traveling and goals. Plans are made 12 months out and tickets are purchased.

Dr. Patel's widowed father-in-law has started taking the families of his three daughters on annual vacations. Cousins are tightly knit and supportive. They have been twice to Africa, Italy, Croatia, Machu Pitchu, Galapagos and many trips to Latin and South America as Tejas is a Spanish speaker. Tejas and Ami always take an annual couples trip and always a family trip of four.

For his practice in Austin, TX, Dr. Patel originally had one practice in an area that became saturated with dentists. He knew he could eventually reach the numbers he wanted but found a different path by seeking another location and working each practice two days a week, usually with an associate. He then actually merged another practice into his second purchase location. He is always open to another merger.

In staffing issues with his purchase and mergers, he learned:

- He would be quicker in letting marginal people go

- Some staff has been awarded an annual increase and were earning far above their pay grade for no increase in skills. Bill had coached him to make the choices for team as a leader and not feel an obligation to hire them for patient loyalty.

- Patients are fine with a new doctor and ok with new team. Hygienists can be a connecting factor if they meet his qualifications.

Dr. Patel currently has a one-day a week associate who works in the same practice when Tejas works. He has had five or more associates in the five years and he has now learned he is seeking dentists who have:

- An openness to learning

- Little desire to own and operate their own practice

- A self-starter personality

He has also learned if the team is trained well and has an ownership mentality, almost any associate can fit in. The team makes it happen.

In his mergers, he wanted to keep as many patients as possible and he did retain a lot by having hygienists continue to see patients and to present more comprehensive dentistry. Both practices were older dentists who referred a lot of work out as well as underdiagnosed for today's dentistry. They had no web presence and just by starting a "crown of the year" club, they were moving forward. After several hygiene visits, the patients were then diagnosed with a more comprehensive treatment plan.

Austin is the state capital, has huge UT-Austin campus of 60K undergraduate students and graduate and professional schools. It is an art, tech and real estate center near the Texas Hill Country. Austin has a personality all its own and is not affected by petroleum industry as Houston. There is a Clear Choice in Austin and their advertising helps all dentists.

In Dr. Patel's two practices, he is specializing in cosmetic dentistry and All on 4 procedures. He is certified in oral sedation and works with an anesthesiologist for IV. Dr. Patel is a Fellow in ICOI for implants. He did his early cosmetic learning at LVI and followed a path of international implant training as live courses were available in the Dominican Republic, Nicaragua, and Brazil. He studied implants with Dr. Virgil Mongalo of liveimplanttraining.com and felt the opportunity to actually participate in surgeries gave him confidence and expertise.

Dr. Patel started maximum use of the internet and social media early on. He has hundreds of YouTube videos which he filmed as "selfies," and were oriented to the emotional side rather than technical dentistry. He is very conscious of marketing. He has three websites and currently is making some professional videos for use on television and the 30 minute Wellness Hour in the Austin area.

One of the many gifts he feels he received with Blatchford Coaching is being a member of the Big Docs group, those collecting $1.6M and above as a solo dentist. Tejas met for the first time at the Big Docs group, Dr. Jayson Tabor of Tennessee and was impressed with his work in volunteering at home clinic as well as in Haiti. Dr. Tabor gave a passionate speech at a Big Docs meeting on the need for volunteer dentistry and before the end of the year, Tejas was on his way to Haiti. It was a life-changing week to be with such dedication of about six dentists working hard and sharing beliefs and promises in life. Tejas is going again this year and he and Dr. Tabor have developed a strong friendship.

Tejas also mentions the value of the closed Facebook connection with all Blatchford clients and how compassionate and helpful others are in lifting you to greater heights.

lakewaysmiles@gmail.com

Playing the Blatchford Game: Dental Mobility

Dental practices are available in the areas that you want to move. Dr. Tejas Patel is a good example of dental mobility. It used to be your first choice for location was it. You planted your feet and stayed. Now, dentistry matches the transitions of America. Moving can be a renewal of energy and focus. Is it the right thing for you?

One of the standards in dental practice has always been to decide where you want to live and hang your shingle. The set rule was that once a dentist established a practice after dental school, he was a definite fixture in that community through retirement years. This paradigm or way of looking at the world is now passé. One of the main reasons is that 44 states now have licensure by credentials. You can move!

Dentists can sell their dental practice and move to another area of town, another area of the state, or another state. Dentists are not stuck in an area just because you own your practice, own your office, own your home. Remember, all of these things were for sale when you established your practice and all will sell again.

I applaud situations where dentists have selected desired areas and after thirty years are still finding the population and economy is remaining stable. Where I am encouraging change is when the dentist established a practice ten or twenty years ago and feels it is no longer as desirable an area but feels stuck. The idea of utilizing his well-honed skills somewhere else wouldn't occur to him because of this old dental paradigm about moving.

Just as America is more transient than ever, dentists can move too. A variety of situations could occur:

- Population mix of the area is changing
- Change in family situations requiring your presence in another area (like older parents)
- Economic base is changing

- Area of concentration (cosmetics or family practice) would be more successful in another area

- Frustration, apathy and boredom are occurring in the practice because of the above

- Desire to practice in a recreation area or new hobby

Benefits of moving could be finding a more promising economic situation where patients see value in your fine work, being close to family in times of need, and selling your practice to someone who now perceives value from his perspective. A change in scenery for a dentist who actually stimulates thinking, growth, and positive energy.

Mental barriers to moving are passing the state boards, selling your practice, finding a suitable practice in the desired area and the stress of moving. Passing another state's board seems like a huge barrier. In actuality, a competent practicing dentist can pass a board. Forty-four states now have licensure by credentials—a valid dental license in one state is acceptable in another state. In addition, there are five regional boards which create opportunity in other states. Feeling stationary or stuck is now a state of mind, rather than an actuality.

The whole transition from preparing your practice for sale to purchasing another practice can be nicely done in 24 months. It is important to know what creates value in your present practice and how can you prepare it for the best sale. A practice has more value when:

- The overhead is 55%, net is 45% or higher

- Skilled stable staff

- Lab bill of 10% or higher

- 50% case acceptance

- Six weeks time off with pay

- Treatment of choice

- Nice facility

- Change – bulk of the dentists are over 50, having graduated when dental schools expanded their numbers in the early 1970s. Some may be looking to retire, some may be wanting to add an additional smaller practice to their existing patient base.

You may perceive your present practice has a declining value because of a changing economic base or population mix. Just as we do not want to prejudge patients, do not prejudge the value of your practice. It is valuable to others for different reasons.

Just as you, practices may be for sale because the doctor is going back to graduate school, has family needs in a different area or feels it is just time to sell. Some doctors may be feeling frustrated at the changes in the dental marketplace and are unwilling to participate any longer. Some practices may be listed with a broker while others are not officially for sale. This is where networking with your peers works well as there are dentists who are either frustrated with the present system, nearing retirement or perceive a different practice environment would be best. A definite decision to sell has not been made. By lunching with possible candidates, you can offer your support should a decision be made. Be the first in line.

There are great success stories in practice sales and there are also horror stories. Our purpose is to help the dentist who wants a move to avoid the heartbreaking pitfalls of some purchases. For help in structuring a practice sale, call Blatchford at 541-389-9088. Learn how to avoid costly pitfalls in purchases and sales.

First, seek a professional broker both for selling your practice and purchasing a new practice. Have the practice appraised. Make certain you are being represented individually. Many times we find the purchasing doctor becomes friendly with the selling doctor's broker. They do not represent you, no matter how much you like them. Find your own representative to look out for you. Look for actual net of the practice by seeking recent tax returns along with profit and loss statements. Net and percentage of lab bill will indicate the real strength of the practice.

A successful practice purchase really requires the help of a smart practice broker. His goal is a win/win for both parties. We coach our doctors to avoid the pitfalls of practice purchase with strong guidelines. A few are:

- Purchase the practice outright and avoid a partnership situation
- Seller leaves the practice with non-compete covenant
- Purchase price is definite at time of sale
- Financing is a complete package and a total buyout is best

A competent broker will help you structure a win/win contract. The selling doctor wins when the financial structure of the sale supports his goals and is able to move into his next project. The buyer wins when the contract structures the sale so there is financial reward from the beginning. He must be in control and able to see benefits from the beginning rather than strictly a payback for the first five years.

Pitfalls we have seen which you can avoid:

- A successful and mature doctor sells and moves to a completely different area somehow perceiving his experience and reputation will be enough to make the new practice successful

- Doctor moving to escape problems in his practice must be aware those leadership, communication or self-esteem issues are moving with you. Seek professional help before taking them with you to the new location

- Moving is a very emotional decision. Doctor wants to move bad enough and does not do homework on demographics and where the transition areas are in the new city.

- Doctor purchases the practice and building. Best to let someone else be the landlord, especially in a transition area

We have seen some real horror stories in practice purchases. We have inherited situations where the selling doctor stays in the practice for an indefinite period of time taking care of any patient he chooses. The purchasing doctor in the meantime, is expected to produce enough to make a comfortable living and repay the selling doctor. A single practice cannot instantly support two full time salaries. This dream can turn into a nightmare quickly. The contract needs to be structured so the selling doctor receives his money and leaves with a non-compete covenant.

Once the practice purchase has been made, you have made the move from one area and successfully purchased in another area. The next immediate step is learning and mastering new skills in enrollment to make certain these new patients are asked questions to discover their needs, really listened to as never before and treatment is actually completed. This is the real value of purchasing a practice—how well you take an already successful practice and make it your own with excellent resulting numbers. Learning case presentation and closing skills are essential to practice success.

If you are not pleased for various reasons with where you are practicing, consider preparing your practice for sale and moving to an area with a fresh approach, new skills and new patients. You are not stuck where you are. You are free to move where ever you desire and take your valuable skills with you. You are at choice to make the new practice successful.

Bill Blatchford, DDS

From the Blatchford Play Book: A Winning Season — Planning, Communicating, Executing

Dr. Patel and his team want a winning season. This is appropriate as Austin is the home of the University of Texas and everyone wants "a winning season."

▶ Define "winning." Will you grow 1% or 10% in what areas?

▶ What is the plan to achieve goals?

▶ What is the benefit for team if we win?

▶ Make available resources of new skills and capital to achieve a winning season

▶ What skills or systems will you implement to make the numbers different from last year?

▶ Make your team meetings effective

▶ Everyone must be at the team meetings, even the kickers and special teams

▶ Communicate the plan, asking for specific accountability from each team member

▶ Break the annual goal into monthly and daily goals. Check at the morning huddle, "where are we, what do we need to do today, who will do it and let us know?"

▶ Practice, practice, practice the skills. Consider a BMW 4 x 4 which is a Blatchford Motivational Workshop four hours every four weeks to master skills. Winning teams have drills again and again.

▶ Can people trust me to do my best?

▶ Am I committed to the dream?

▶ Do I care about my team?

▶ There must be loyalty up and down the line

▶ What can we learn from this?

4

KING OF EPHRATA

Dr. Brian Jacobsen

Seeking the sun, Brian and his family came to Ephrata, WA, population 7900, where they now enjoy 300+ days of sunshine a year and rainfall totals similar to Phoenix. He knows you've never heard of Ephrata, and that's just the way he likes it. Though he never would've considered it when he first arrived, with Blatchford coaching and encouragement, he was able to pursue an incredible opportunity by purchasing and combining two dental practices. Soon after that, at a Peak Performance Seminar, Bill dubbed him "The King of Ephrata," and the rest is history. With his wife, Laura, they are raising three children. They are making a great effort to build confidence and love with each child. His oldest is William, and together, they do a weekly hike where they enjoy finding cool rock formations, offroading their FJ cruiser, chocolate, and the music of Josh Groban, love riding their tandem bicycle to his weekly breakfast with Dad. Emily, their daughter, has a weekly dessert time with Dad. She usually wants to take the convertible . . . and he bravely listens to her Taylor Swift. His youngest, Andrew, enjoys a weekly breadfast with Dad.

Though this is a dental business book, for Brian, it is more about lifestyle. "Currently, I'm at the tail end of three-and-a-half weeks off and we certainly jammed it full of fun. The family and I headed to Florida, went to Legoland, on a four-day Disney cruise with four other Blatchford Docs and families, went to Kennedy Space Center, did three days of Harry Potter and other rides at Universal, came home, made two trips to a great Chelan waterpark, visited a new museum, hiked in the Columbia River Gorge and Lava Canyon at Mt. St. Helens, and went to a concert. Following Blatchford's advice on time-off has really helped me to reconnect with friends, family, and places I've loved in the past. I have really changed my mentality and my perspective toward work and time off. I've put a lot of work into having the right team and we work hard and efficiently when in the office...so we can thoroughly enjoy other aspects of life when we're not. In many ways, it's like I've gotten my (relatively) carefree pre-dental life back...but better in so many ways!"

Brian is continually a surprise. He is quiet and thoughtful but also has a fun sense of humor and a wide variety of interests. Brian grew up in rainy Astoria, Oregon, and he returned there for eight years as an associate. Although he is a "Goonie" through and through, Brian and his family tired of drear and dampness and sought sunshine and a change of pace east of the Cascades. A practice became available in Ephrata. He initially was pleased with working 180 days for $700K collections and 6.5 staff. Brian felt like he was running by the seat of his pants, though, with inconsistent customer service and frequent difficulty staying on schedule. He felt his patients owned him. He took CE but it usually didn't convert into financial success. He was scared and worried he might have the wrong mindset for success. He was playing the lean game not to lose rather than thinking big.

Brian has always felt you become like the people you hang with. So, he decided he wanted to hang around with busy accomplished dentists. In spite of the hour commute each way, he joined a Spear

Study Club even though he had not taken any Spear classes. One doctor, Matt Fluegge, quickly stood out to him. He arrived via a variety of cool trucks and motorcycles, seemed to have many days off and lots of different hobbies to pursue on them and he had impressive confidence, knowledge and dedication to his family. Brian says "It was my *Pursuit of Happyness* moment with Matt playing the role of the stockbroker in the Ferrari. When I asked, 'What do you do and how do you do it?', his reply was 'Hire Blatchford and do what he says'."

When joining Blatchford, Brian mentioned there was a practice for sale in Ephrata but felt he couldn't qualify as it was larger then his, producing about $1.1M with no insurance. Shortly after he joined Blatchford, we coached him through this purchase. This made him one of just two full-time dentists in his town. Shortly thereafter, he went out-of-network with Delta, his only insurance—a huge decision. He also recently completed the purchase of the far-superior building in which he practices.

While Brian admits it has not always been easy, the results have been spectacular. With direction and encouragement from Bill, Christina and consultant Kaye Puccetti, the King of Ephrata has:

- Added CEREC, dental sleep medicine, oral sedation and early third molar extractions
- Has 13 weeks of time off, working M, T and Th (128 patient care days a year)
- More than doubled daily production and achieved $1.2M a year with 52% overhead
- Created goals of greater efficiency per hour and increased health and fitness

Dr. Jacobsen embraces the Blatchford philosophy "if something is being done, it is probably possible," meaning "I can do it, too." Post-merger, he started noticing he was doing larger cases and more same-day dentistry. He still does bill insurance but has no relationship with them.

He continues to brand himself though, with videos, newspaper articles, presentations, mailers and even has a billboard.

He is now a stronger leader and has worked to form a great team with positive attitudes who each bonus between $500 and $1400 per period. His team of five is comprised of one in front, one assistant, a rover, and two hygienists. Having the right team, being on guaranteed pay per pay period, and implementing the Blatchford bonus system has resulted in a much higher degree of ownership.

Dr. Jacobsen is in Blatchford CONNECTION, the graduate level, and stays in touch monthly. He recalls a time where he was wrestling with a decision regarding a team member and took the opportunity to be on three hours of a Network call (these one-hour calls coincide with lunchtime in the three US time zones . . . and he stayed on the whole time). By the end of the call, with a number of doctors and Blatchford consultants chiming in, he knew what he had to do: let the person go that very day. Another benefit of Blatchford CONNECTION is that Brian also has become networked with successful dentists all over the country through the closed Blatchford Facebook forum called Dental IQ.

He feels now the team drives the practice forward together. Even patients comment on the pleasant positive attitude. Brian and his team find everything runs smoother with their effective morning meetings and a PM huddles. Post-op calls have also done wonders to boost the reputation of the practice in the community.

He learned sleep apnea with Dr. Steven Greenman's online course and it resonated with him as Brian is being treated for apnea with an oral appliance. With Blatchford encouragement, he now has CEREC and offers sedation (oral . . . so far). He seeks to differentiate himself by being capable of full service. He recently did John Wayland's third molar course and is scheduled for Misch's implant series in Los Angeles.

Dr. Jacobsen says, "As I followed and applied advice from Bill and Christina, I essentially walked into my dream home, dream car, dream piano, dream vacations, and I have the time to enjoy them with those I love."

Brian has learned to dream again and his new goal is to walk on the moon. Space will suffice, but he really wants the moon. He is very excited about seeing all three Space Shuttles in one year. Brian shares "When I was 12, I went to Space Camp and wanted to be an astronaut. This was about the time my vision got worse and I had to get glasses. I found out that, with glasses, I wouldn't get to fly the Shuttle or be the Mission Commander. Plus, I was a late bloomer and I grew up a scrawny, allergic, asthmatic kid who basically stayed indoors playing Atari and Legos. The seeming impossibility of the physical fitness requirements for being an astronaut put the nail in the coffin of my dream. But just in the past year, my trips with the Blatchfords have taken me back to my dreams! On my first bike trip with them, a near-hurricane created some indoor time in the DC area. So, we visited the Udvar-Hazy Center near Dulles Field and saw the Space Shuttle Discovery. The dream was sparked again after another Blatchford Adventure. At Bill's encouragement, my family and I visited Kennedy Space Center which now features the Shuttle Atlantis! These experiences, combined with Bill's contagious enthusiasm for abundance, space travel, and technology creating a better future, has led to a re-emergence of my dream! Now it is **really** a spark, and I have tickets to see the Shuttle Endeavour to feed it even more! It is my belief that I will have the opportunity to go to space, if not the moon, in my lifetime. This motivates me to take good care of myself and to keep working harder and smarter in my dental practice to make sure I can fund it."

The King of Ephrata feels it is truly an honor and a privilege to be in *Bringing Your 'A' Game 2.0*. "Blatchford has been invaluable in helping me change the course of my practice, my family and my life. If you have the courage to be teachable and take action, working with Blatchford will absolutely be the best investment you will ever make."

drbrianjacobsen@gmail.com

Brian, age 12, at Space Camp

Brian and Laura

Can you hear the music?

Arrrgh! Pirates on the Disney Cruise

The King and hs TEAM

Blatchford Game Plan
Assessing Your Insurance Dependence

Dr. Jacobsen originally was a Delta provider in Ephrata. When Brian purchased his second practice which was larger than his first, the selling doctor was not a Delta provider. Brian made the big decision, with Blatchford encouragement, to be completely fee for service.

Continued profitability is important. It is one of the main reasons you chose dentistry. In changing economic conditions, is it feasible for a dentist to become a non-provider of insurance? If you continued to be a provider during the last ten years of boom economy, are you forever tied to insurance? If I make changes, how will it affect my profitability?

Insurance decisions are emotional. And yet, it is fiscally irresponsible to make a decision, strictly on an emotional level, which will greatly affect your profitability. It takes an emotional and financial assessment and a solid plan of action.

On an emotional level, you need introspection to discover why you want to be a non-provider. Know these reasons. What is the purpose of coming to work each day? What are you and your staff trying to accomplish? If words arrive like excellence, results, choices, freedom, responsibility, how then does insurance support fit for you? In your opinion, how can you best provide excellence, freedom of choice?

You decide, for that decision is based on your own ethical standards. The financial assessment is simply numbers. Find out your percentage of collections from insurance. It does not matter the number of patients on insurance. You need to know the amount of treatment being accepted in your office and supported by insurance. If you have over 50% of your collections coming from insurance, you still have several choices. You need to plan for the worst. If 50% of your practice left, would you still be operating?

One choice is to continue as you are and keep challenging fees and diagnosis. Another choice is to establish an "insurance independence" date, for example July 4, several years from now. The goal is to change the mix of treatment being offered in your practice from the present "Crown of the Year" Club, "just fix the worst one," or "just do what my insurance will cover." Moving from Crown of the Year Club to offering more optional treatment requires new sales skills. This is no pressure sales where you ask the patient questions. If you have a 50% insurance collection, you and your staff, as well as your patients, are mentally tied to insurance. It is on your mind all the time and you are aware of each patient's insurance, thinking there is no other path.

As you change the mix of treatment offered, your goal is to show a decrease in insurance dependence. You need to become more skilled in relationships, selling rather than telling and attracting patients to your practice who see value in work beyond their insurance maximums. Learn how to create value for treatment not covered by insurance. Ask your patients what benefits or advantages they see in healthy teeth and smiles.

If you choose to become a non-provider of insurance, your plan for profitability must include the increasing of your marketing and sales skills and budget. You must fill the void that insurance companies have marketed for you by signing with employers who encouraged their employees to seek your regular care. Insurance has provided your sales. If you use the same sales technology when selling optional care, it will not be successful. An insurance sale is "let's preauthorize this," "let's fix the worst two" with the expected response of "I'll do what my insurance covers."

Evaluate your ability to become a non-provider by examining your own numbers. Plan for that percentage of your practice to leave. If that percentage of treatment left your practice, where would you be? Change the mix of treatment to more optional care and make a plan for learning marketing and sales.

Bill Blatchford, DDS

From the Blatchford Play Book:
Creating A Fan Club

Because Dr. Jacobsen is fee for service, he continues to brand his practice to create a fan club, yes, even for the King of Ephrata.

➤ Doctor and hygienist call your patients at night

➤ Respect your guests' time, in on time and out on time

➤ Develop deep relationships with your patients which creates trust

➤ People will buy from you because they trust you. Show your guests you care, an important element in building friendships

➤ Ask questions of them; make them the focus of the conversation. Sadly, people aren't really interested in you, your political opinions or your cat

➤ Be generous, give guests a nice bag of "goodies" from their dental visit

➤ Think of guests often on birthdays, different holidays like Thanksgiving, New Years, Flag Day

➤ Create email newsletters to continue contact with your guests

➤ Fill newsletters with human interest stories, not about your new laser

➤ Have all the creature comforts of a spa

➤ Have a full complement of juice, coffee, soups, teas

➤ Think about serving espresso with hot cookies

➤ Know the latest events in guests' lives like graduations, births, travel, etc.

➤ Photography is a real practice builder. Create a photo studio in one operatory or consult room.

➤ Learn case presentation skills to involve your guests in sharing their dreams

➤ Give latte gift certificates

5

SUCCESSFUL MERGER

Dr. Steve Sirin

Dr. Steve Sirin and his team did the ultimate merger. In 2015, Steve originally heard Bill speak at the AACD's annual gathering, hosted in San Francisco that year.

The salient point Steve heard Bill make is that mergers are the least expensive way to acquire new patients. Consider how much one spends on marketing, where no one can really be sure how much good it's doing.

If one takes one's monthly marketing expenses, plus a little extra, and uses that money to instead make payments toward the purchase of another practice of the right size, a dentist can acquire new patients while being able to discern the actual costs—costs that are considerably lower than if one acquires patients through traditional marketing practices such as direct mail and assurances by online marketing companies that they know how to game search engine algorithms.

Steve knew he was spending a lot on marketing, yet was not really moving forward. His practice is fee-for-service, so he was aiming at a select group.

When Steve returned home to Elgin, Illinois, he called brokers and found that a dentist whom he had met at a professional gathering more than a year earlier, was wanting to retire. The aspiring retiree needed only to find a dentist to whom he would feel comfortable turning over patients with whom he had career-long relationships.

Dr. Sirin confided in Bill Blatchford that he felt his practice had excess capacity. Steve had more chairs than patients to keep them full.

Steve's first practice had four dated treatment rooms in an office condominium. The practice Steve was considering was in a free-standing building two miles away. The building was comprised of two suites, and the selling doctor owned them both. Perfect, Steve thought. Steve bought the entire 3,200-square-foot building and now has six operatories and a concept in the works that features eight operatories plus a consult room that would give his patients a private place to discuss their care with Dr. Sirin and their financial arrangements with his office manager.

Steve and his team were able to move equipment and records, folding the two practices together into the free-standing facility. Steve anticipates putting the vacated office space on the market within a year.

After a few anxious moments in the first couple of weeks, Dr. Sirin said, "The merger worked better than I ever dreamed."

Kudos to Dr. Brad Bramen, Bill and consultant Nanci Granahan for coaching him on the purchase, on how to combine staff into a new, cohesive unit and on merging both patient bases.

The Blatchford group changed the mindsets of both the doctor and the team.

Hygiene is always a consideration for doctors merging practices. Steve originally had 6.5 days of hygiene each week, and now has 12 days. When Steve has triple hygiene scheduled, they focus on time management and teamwork in diagnosis. Steve's team tries to have perio in the morning so Steve can make his doctor production goals. His hygienists are now scheduling patients, plus they are accepting hygiene payments at the end of appointments in their operatories. Patients love it, as does Steve's office manager, Mary Carol.

Steve knows he has lost some patients. Nonetheless, the schedule remains busy. Steve now has many patients vying for appointments. When someone misses his or her hygiene appointment, Steve's team doesn't call again.

Steve made both of his existing hygienists full-time and added a third full-time hygienist who had been working for the retiring dentist. Steve actually intended to hire the receptionist at the practice he bought, but she chose not to stay. The low-tech receptionist took with her decades of institutional knowledge and left behind an out-of-date Rolodex that did not match the office's archaic yellow billing sheets or recall cards as well as a computer used for the sole purpose of submitting bills electronically.

Steve's talented office manager, Mary Carol, accepted the challenge to pull all the patient information together and was exuberant when she eventually prevailed. Steve's mom, and even Mary Carol's retired mother, came in to help with data entry.

Immediately after the merger, Dr. Sirin and his new team increased production by 41%, which is about what he had anticipated. What Steve hadn't anticipated is that, over the subsequent months, his production would continue to steadily increase as he incorporated Blatchford principles into his office management. Ten months into the Blatchford program, his team's production had increased by 79% compared with pre-merger production.

At the same time, Steve and his team reduced the number of days they will work by 41 days to 180 days in 2016 from 221 days in 2015.

When Bill met Steve at his summit, Bill commented, "This boy needs to learn to have fun." Dr. Sirin agreed.

He and his partner accepted American Airlines' "Platinum Challenge." They then tasked themselves to fly enough in the following to maintain platinum status. They went to California twice, Texas, and on vacations to the tiny Dutch island of Curaçao in the Caribbean, Barcelona, Spain and Japan—more than enough to satisfy their goal.

A few months before signing up with Blatchford Solutions, Steve and his partner had planned a trip to Maui for their one annual vacation. A few days before they planned to leave, his partner broke his hip, forcing them to cancel the trip. Steve was so looking forward to this vacation. He was shocked to realize how much he needed that planned time off to recoup and reinvent. He feels that with the Blatchford vacation schedule, he never feels drained going to work.

"This past year has been so amazing both personally and professionally," Dr. Sirin said. I never expected anyone could improve my life like Blatchford. It has exceeded my most indulgent expectations. I am excited every day. I feel I am growing as a dentist, as a team and in life.

Next year, Steve is looking forward to starting Kois comprehensive restorative courses in the new year, further relaxation in the surf and on the brown sugar sands of Maui's beaches and is planning an autumn driving vacation through France and Germany, where he will trade in his BMW 4 Series for a 5 Series through BMW's European Delivery program. You go, Steve!

www.drsirin.com

Blatchford Game Plan
Pareto Principle — The 80/20 Rule

Dr. Sirin is using this statistical analysis to merge two practices. He wants to watch the top 20% of his patients emerge during this year. Pareto's Principle is most useful in dentistry as the result is greater efficiency in concentrating on those who enjoy you and your services as opposed to crying over those bottom 20% who cause 80% of your headaches. *

Pareto's Law (the 80/20 Rule) has been effectively used for years by big business in marketing and sales. The 80/20 Rule is a fascinating percentage which applies to so many areas of our lives and which nobody can explain why it continues to occur. It really is the secret to success by achieving more with less.

We coach our Doctors and staffs in sales, ask questions so your guest or patient speaks 80% of the time. Conversely, if staff and Doctor are "educating" 80% of the conversation, you will talk your way out of a sale 80% of the time.

We receive 80% of our headaches, complaints and cancellations from 20% of our patients. These are patients who don't see value in what we have to offer. We create "office policy" for all because of the problem few. Your worst patients have then helped you create a pessimistic practice, rather than one of optimism and trust.

A computer survey will show you produce 80% of your production from 20% of the patients. Look carefully at the top 20% of those patients last year. Who are they? What did they elect to purchase in your office? Why are they attracted to you? What can you learn from this exercise? Be curious and study this magic 20%. Focus and concentrate on replicating that behavior.

The 80/20 rule of marketplace consumption is in every industry. Airlines know they make 80% of profit from 20% of fliers. These business travelers and frequent fliers are awarded with extra perks, bigger seats, upgrades and service. Airlines know they do not make their profits from a family traveling to Disneyland once a year.

Dentists tend to ignore the 80/20 rule because we are trying to please everybody all the time. Our percentages are reversed. We want patients to accept what we feel they need. We work hard to reverse the thinking of the emergency patient who is demanding of our time every three years.

We struggle to diagnose above insurance maximums. Frustrated, we quit trying. We fill our hygiene schedule with any "meat in the seat." Upon cancellation, we give them other immediate choices. We devalue our own work to cater to the 80% who are not our best patients.

In our Custom Coaching Program, we designate patients as A, B and C. The majority of your patients are A patients who faithfully remember your birthday, bring tomatoes from their garden, keep their appointments, pay on time and refer people just like them. Conversely, C patients are the unfaithful who have no tomatoes, only come when it is convenient and refer friends just like them. These are the bottom 20% who create practice pain.

B patients just take up space. Their attention is sporadic. We want all A patients but tend to create policies and treat people as if they are C's.

Watch for indications you and your staff may be catering to the B and C patients.

- Is insurance mentioned by you in the initial phone conversation?

- Health history in mail prior to first appointment relationship opportunity?

- Is money mentioned in the initial phone call?

- Is respect for time a problem in your office?

- Does a new patient sit alone in "waiting room" completing forms?

- Is one of your first questions, "do you have any concerns today?"

- Is finding insurance information a priority before doctor sees a patient?

- Are you insurance experts on codes, fee structures and maximums?

If you answered yes to above, you have geared your practice for average. In order to cater to the top 20%, a clear sense of leadership and passion for change must be communicated and demonstrated. Stop doing the things that make you average and shift to being extraordinary. Attitude is a big factor. If you see yourself in the average 80%, unable to break out, stuck in a scheduling quagmire and insurance diagnosis paralysis, you will stay in the 80%.

Find yourself a coach who can turn that attitude into winning. As Lou Holtz says in a commercial, "Son, there is no such thing as just a sales call. You need a fight song."

*Another way to discover the top 20% of your patients is to ask each staff member to list their 100 favorite patients based on attitude, relationship, fun, commitment, etc. Then merge the list into the team's 100 top patients. Check this 100 list against your computer survey of the top 20% who account for 80% of your income. There will be a great correlation of the two lists. Then study those people. Who are they? Where do they work and live? Why do they see value in your services? These are the top 20% of people who make your life wonderful. How can you thank them and honor them? Also, how can you duplicate them? How can we attract more of them?

Bill Blatchford, DDS

From the Blatchford Play Book: Winning Play

Dr. Sirin is the leader of a winning team. Winning teams practice for any possibility and go full out all the time because they never know which one of the 100 plays or more in a football game will be the deciding play.

▶ There is no such thing as a "sure thing."

▶ Play hard and focused on every play; this may be the one.

▶ Hard work makes dreams come true

▶ Time & efficiency is important, time your procedures, learn efficiency

▶ Practice, practice, practice

▶ Let staff enroll the dentistry

▶ Doctor tells the patient the fees

▶ Stop blaming others, take responsibility for your life.

▶ In learning new skills, it will always feel downright phony at first. Stick with it and it will be uncomfortable sometimes, then comfortable and finally integrated

▶ Put strong systems in place in your practice which will tide you in good times and not so good times

▶ Staff for what you are presently doing, not what you hope to do in five years

▶ The important thing is to know you've tried your very hardest, have given 100% on every play.

▶ Being successful is doing your best

▶ Don't be known as the one who could have or should have but as one that did.

▶ A great player must rise to the occasion and turn the game around on his own

▶ Choose winning players based on attitude

▶ Winning teams practice harder than they play

6

STATE OF GRACE

Dr. Laura Aeschlimann

A busy pediatric dentist in Sioux Falls, SD, Laura Dykstra Aeschlimann is leading the way with over 50% of American females being the principal bread-winner for their family. Called the Big Switch, females are the ones earning the money and thus, the male becomes the primary caretaker of the children and is in charge of executing the majority of the duties in the home.

Laura owns one of only two pediatric practices in Sioux Falls, SD, a city of 175,000 with 75,000 more in the surrounding area. She knew from a young age she wanted to work solely with children, and she is as busy as she would like in her three-year-old start-from-scratch practice. She chose dentistry early in life because she always had good experiences as a child going to the dentist. When her front teeth grew in crowded and her four lower primary incisors had to be extracted, her mom had the teeth bronzed and returned to little 6-year-old Laura framed and mounted along with a certificate from the Tooth Fairy. In the fifth grade, she had a cleaning and remembers consciously realizing though other dental staff did the majority of the work, it was the dentist who received the respect for his knowledge and skills and was the owner of the practice.

By high school, she had already told all her family and friends for years that her goal was to become a dentist, so she was then determined and just stubborn and dedicated enough to follow through with that career plan. She was accepted into the University of Minnesota Dental School after just three years of pre-requisites at South Dakota State. She followed that with her pediatric training at University of Nebraska Medical Center in Omaha. Laura then served as Chief of Pediatric Dentistry while stationed at Kadena Air Base in Okinawa, Japan after the completion of her dental training. During dental school Laura had applied for and accepted a Health Professionals Scholarship Program (HPSP) scholarship from the USAF which paid for three years of dental school tuition and expenses then required Laura to serve five years Reserves and three years active duty in the military.

While completing her pediatric residency in Omaha, she met a young man, Chad, at a wedding dance, and two weeks before leaving her family and country, they were married. Laura went to Commissioned Officer Training just days after their nuptials, and six weeks later the newlyweds were reunited in Japan. Moving away for three years helped them form a strong married relationship as they created their own vision and culture. They had to rely deeply on one another for friendship and support since friends and family were all a half-a-world away and even on a time zone that was completely opposite of their own.

Her husband Chad was trained in sports fitness management in college. In Japan, he worked as a substitute teacher for the first two of the three years they were stationed there. At the start of the third year, their son Tanner was born. As Tanner grew, he was diagnosed as special needs including seizures, autism, and developmental delays. How very fortunate Chad could and wanted to care for their son at this time and in the years to come. Over the years, they have sought specialists in Texas, Florida, and Minnesota, as well as have found terrific medical, therapy, and educational care right in Sioux Falls. Tanner, now 10 years old, is non-verbal, tube-fed, and goes to a specialty day school in Sioux Falls for his educational and therapy needs.

With the female being the primary breadwinner in their family, Chad's role is so very important as he is able to get Tanner off to school in the morning and be there when he gets home after school as well as get him to many doctors appointments, allowing Laura to work the hours she needs and wants as a pediatric dentist. She is able to focus on dentistry while at work and then focus completely at home when at home with her family. Chad is also able to manage the finances in both their home and at the dental office. He has time during the day while Tanner is at school to pursue both his entrepreneurial ventures and his hobbies.

When Laura, Chad, and Tanner returned to the States in 2007, she associated for nearly five years before deciding that her practice philosophy and vision for her career and life required her to resign from her associateship and to start her own practice. She and Chad had been following the Dave Ramsey principles for their finances and as a result, she was able to quit her part-time associate job and spend the next six months living off of their "emergency fund" as they designed and built the building, and prepared for the opening of her newly created pediatric dental practice: ABC Pediatric Dentistry.

In dental school, Laura had the opportunity to participate in numerous mission trips, one of her passions. In private practice, mission trips were available but not always convenient to add into an already busy practice and personal life schedule. Three years ago, though, Laura decided it was time to MAKE TIME for missions again and went on a mission trip to Jamaica with her husband, mom, and some friends from dental school. One of the participants was a new acquaintance, a Blatchford client, Dr. Angie Bauer Williams. They discussed what a positive difference Blatchford Solutions made in Angie's life and the guidance she had received that made the practice of dentistry so much more fulfilling with the coaching of Drs. Bill and Christina and Team. Angie had found through their coaching, things Laura, too, had been looking for: ways to create more time out of the office, how to put together a stellar Team who would provide great care and support one another in cultivating a fun, happy environment, and how to incorporate doctor admin time into the work week instead of evenings and weekends.

Laura came home from that mission trip and watched every "Mornings with Blatchfords," made notes, and even had Chad watch, too. She called Dr. Lori Kerber, a Blatchford pediatric dentist, and the recorded reply from Dr. Kerber was so inspiring to Laura, she contacted Blatchford to begin a new, improved chapter in her life and practice.

Dr. Aeschlimann now has a great Team who believe in the vision she has which has reduced the stress level. She feels working with Blatchford is such a blessing. She is pleased Blatchford has created a phone conference for pediatric dentists to share their concerns and accomplishments. She loves the Dental IQ Facebook group as an invaluable resource and support. Her pedo practice has great demand. The practice in which she first associated has just closed their doors and that doctor, her mentor, retired. Laura was busy enough already, so she was not interested in a purchase of that practice or those patients, desiring to continue to be available for her current patients of record and for referrals from general dentists. She is not interested in hiring an associate as her vision is to continue to practice as a sole provider with a small but dedicated Team. The other pedo practice in the city has five male dentists. She is not only the only female pediatric dentist in the area, she is also the only pediatric dentist who allows parents the choice to come back and be with their child during all appointments.

Because the demand for her services is great, she does minimal marketing but continues to brand herself, mostly by proving top quality care and customer service. ABC Pediatric Dentistry's tag line is "Compassionate Dental Care for Kids." Her Team does hand-written thank you notes for referrals and sends out first visit photos with personalized new patient cards to the little patients. They have a strong website and lots of positive Facebook reviews. When she first moved back to South

Dakota, Laura realized she missed the dental school camaraderie of like-minded dentists so she created a group of female dental peers to gather on a regular basis. They now know her well and refer to her. It was not her motive to create such a group for generate referrals, yet it has naturally created positive, sincere relationships within the local dental community.

Laura's goal is to enjoy the practice of pediatric dentistry her entire career and avoid burnout. She'd like to have the financial freedom in her mid-50s to have the option to retire early if she would choose someday, or to be able to provide more donated dentistry later in her career. The Aeschlimanns are strong in their Christian faith and want to use their resources, gifts, and talents to serve others. They choose to "live like no one else so they can live like no one else" – to quote Dave Ramsey. She and Chad know life can be short and are not waiting until retirement to live a full life. They are just finishing building their dream home and have years ago paid off all of their combined thirteen years of school debt. Laura is most appreciative of Blatchford's business coaching which has reinvigorated her to continue to strive ever onward with her visions for her career and life goals.

www.drabcdental.com

Laura, husband Chad and son Tanner

Laura and son Tanner

Laura and husband Chad

Laura on her Jamaican mission as a pediatric dentist

Laura and her dream home, nearly finished

Blatchford Game Plan: Romancing the Patient

In changing times, people are seeking security. They want to feel known, needed and that you care about them. Building these relationships is a factor of caring, time and respect. In a way, building a relationship with patients is like a romance. Relationships are the most important quality, which keeps clients and friends mutually attracted. It is that element of trust which bonds two people together.

Because each being is so precious, high priorities should be placed on building solid relationships. Many books have been written about romance and attracting the positive attention of that special someone. To be an interesting person, very simply you must be interested in others. Ask questions. These social skills, communication and curiosity can be learned.

Because 20% of Americans move each year, your new patient goal needs to replace that 20% plus a factor for growth. When we find a practice gathering five new patients a month, the question is, "What are you doing to keep people away?" Where is the romance in your dental office?

Demonstrating genuine caring, quality time and real respect can start with the initial phone call. This is where the romance starts. A warm personal response before the second ring will gather notice. STOP whatever else you are doing and focus on your new friend. Though you answer the phone two hundred times a day, recreate newness. Try, "Thank you for calling Vitality Dental. It is a great day to be pampered. This is Toni and I can help you." This is a surprising and excellent way to start a new relationship.

Your job is to find their name early and use it often. Upon making a timely appointment (within the next several working days), ask of their expectations for the appointment. As in a romance, a definite "no-no" would be to ask, "When was the last time…?" or "Do you have insurance?" Ask your new friend, "Who may we thank for referring you?" Have printed directions to your office ready to fax or email. In preparation for the appointment, invite the patient to visit the office's website. To further enhance the new relationship, you can ask them for a favor. The response is always positive. Your question might be, "Between now and next Tuesday, will you think about what you like best about your smile and what you dislike about your smile?"

Upon arrival at your office how would you like to be treated on a blind date? How do you make them feel important? How do you acknowledge them for their brilliance in calling your office? When your new friend arrives, greet them at the door by name with a warm handshake.

On a first date, you would not want to gather information, which sounded like you were interested in their financial history or family medical secrets. Ask person to person only the medical information you need to complete a prophy in hygiene. They have not asked you for any other treatment at this time.

You can create a practice culture where strangers become friends, and friends become clients, by enveloping them in a sincere and immediate friendship. You are the receptacle for their thoughts and feelings. Very little is shared about yourself.

In demonstrating care, time and respect, create new agreements for patient protocol, which are akin to rules of romance:

- Never leave your guest alone

- Follow-through by doing what you promised you would do

- Create a renewed respect for time with patients being seen and able to depart on time

Think of these first appointments as opportunities to romance your clients. Review the atmosphere and logistics to shift from clinical order takers to an atmosphere of romance. Make people feel needed and wanted as a person, not just a set of teeth.

Bill Blatchford, DDS

From the Blatchford Play Book:
Leave Something Behind

Dr. Laura Aeschlimann sees dentistry and her life as a "giver." Yes, she is profitable and she is grateful. She is also conscious that she has skills and financial abilities which others do not possess. Dentists and teams can make a difference for others by being a mentor, creating an opportunity for someone less able and to have choices for themselves and others.

► Help young people get started

► Be a mentor in something you have passion

► Share your knowledge and experience

► Helping others helps yourself

► Consider teaching in some form

► Be a giver, not a taker

► Be a hero to someone

► Set a lofty example as a rich bequest of scholarships, endowments, trusts

► Do something meaningful for others

► Look for ways to share your skills in the community of man

► Encourage your team to volunteer

► Establish quarterly "giving days" to do dentistry for those who are in the gaposis between insurance and welfare

► How much is enough? How will you give back? What is your plan?

7

FROM THE BEGINNING

Drs. Tom and Tamara Fernandes and Dr. Adam Kirkpatrick

Drs. Fernandez

It is such a pleasure to work with newly graduated doctors before different decisions and paths are chosen. Tom and Tamara are University of Pacific Dental School graduates and have benefited greatly from Blatchford coaching. Tom and Tamara originally met as undergrads singing in the premier undergraduate choir at the University of Arizona.

They practice together in South Lake Tahoe, CA and now actually have an additional practice in Stateline NV, which is right across the state border and only six miles away! They initially worked with Tamara's father in a high end Sedona, AZ practice and eventually realized, there was not enough work for three doctors. Their U of P classmate is Adam Kirkpatrick who said, "Before you make a move, call Blatchford Solutions." They did and it has been a real pleasure to help these two find their niche and be on a path of prosperity from the beginning.

Mom and Dad to two—a toddler and a baby—Tom and Tamara initially purchased two smaller practices in the area and continued to work in them for a year, knowing they were going to merge into one.

Soon after merging the original two practices into one, along came another practice opportunity across the state line and they now have two thriving practices six miles apart. To the locals, six miles seems like a long way, and crossing the state border represents a mental hurdle. Eventually, they want to find a single facility in between and operate out of one location.

Their practices are Fee for Service, though working with all insurances, if possible. The last practice purchase was perfect, but it was "right practice, right price, wrong time", as Tamara was six months pregnant when they found the practice! Tamara was planning on taking 8-10 weeks off with maternity leave and the selling doctor was willing to stay for six months to make it work.

Tom and Tamara introduced the Blatchford concepts and systems slowly with the new team. They did find most of the staff in this second practice eventually retired with the doctor, and this was beneficial for everyone.

Both work Monday, Tuesday and Wednesday, trading practices. Patients know both doctors and are comfortable. They have a different drawing area for each practice. They are on the same page for leadership. Tom is more vocal,yet, they feel they have the same answer.

They are interested in more denture patients. Their NP numbers are an impressive 30-40 a month as Tyson Steele does their marketing. They have a vision of being THE dentists for families in the area. They want to do the best dentistry people can afford, and they want to be experts in helping people afford the care they want and need. The Fernandes' office is one of the most up to date in the area. They envision a One Stop Shop where they refer very little. Their vision for their brand is for every patient to have a phenomenal dental experience, regardless of the level of care they need. Tom was one of five Blatchford Doctors who took an IV course from Dr. John Weyland (westernsurgicaland-sedation.com) and they were a positive force in the course and made such an impact, one of their classmates became a new Blatchford client.

They are taking eight weeks off this year and 10-11 weeks next year. They love that they have dinner together every night and have the ability to set their own schedules.

Tahoe is new to them, too, and they enjoy discovering all things about the area with small roadtrips and adventures. They are involved in community planning so everything is possible in the future. Tom and Tamara love Tahoe and want to foster change. There are new businesses and updates. It is a tough housing market with many good properties tied up with rentals.

Because Tom and Tamara started with Blatchford Coaching from the beginning, they observe some classmates making their way through some purchases, PPO's and dental mills. They feel very fortunate to be together, working on a definite path of debt reduction with practice success.

www.laketahoedental.com
www.laketahoeimplantdentist.com

*Tamara and Tom
competing in the
Tough Mudder
Mud Run*

Dr. Kirkpatrick

Adam, his wife Kelsie and three little Kirkpatricks have found their dream home on a hobby farm of five acres, year-round creek, forest acreage, a hill with a tremendous view, lots of fire pits and a full shop.

What could be better?

Dr. Kirkpatrick is a University of the Pacific graduate who is in love with his dental school. Dr. Art Dugoni instilled a culture of respect with "humanism" as a basis. "Even as a first year student," Adam says, "you are called 'doctor' and told repeatedly 'you are smart and worthy.' This helped set the professional stage for me and what kind of doctor I want to be." He is grateful that they also fostered a supportive environment for his wife while he was in school and they even have a psychologist on staff. Adam gave an example of a time in school when he gave the $20 he had earned by tutoring another student to the alumni association. For that, Dr. Dugoni took Adam to lunch in a very nice SF restaurant and a year later, Dr. Dugoni stopped Adam in the hall and asked about his wife, Kelsie. "I was so impressed that such a busy and important man would remember details about me and my life." Adam continues to be impressed with Dr. Dugoni and the progress of his alma mater.

Another mentor for Adam has been his father, Dr. Kim Kutsch who practices nearby in Albany, OR. When Adam was 12, his mother married Kim. Adam says, "He is a good man, loves dentistry, is smart, kind and inquisitive." He took Adam to a lecture and Adam could see Kim's passion for dentistry. Adam went to OHSU dental camp in high school and caught that passion for dentistry as his own. Adam loves that he can use chemistry, physics, and his "nerdy science" side at work, while also developing leadership skills, team building, and being continually challenged. He loves working with people and finds joy in his profession. Kutsch / Kirkpatrick family gatherings always have a dental component with his brother, Carson, also a dentist and other dental connections in their family. "It's such an interesting profession, there's always something new to talk about." And Adam and Carson have more than the normal amount of family gatherings together, as these brothers married sisters Kelsie and Hayley.

Adam is the first dentist to seek Blatchford counsel straight out of dental school. He was encouraged by family members and Adam is a very optimistic and enthusiastic being. "I knew I wanted to be the best dentist and have the best practice I could have, so I figured I would just start out with the right coaching team to help me get there faster. Many of the things that I have learned in working with the Blatchford team would have taken me my whole career to learn. I was lucky enough to be able to avoid some of the pitfalls that some of my classmates have made." He himself has referred three or more dentists to our program, people he sat next to in lecture and was wearing his seat out with enthusiasm.

Lebanon, OR is mid-Willamette Valley near I-5 with a little over 16,000 in population. It is a former mill town, written off at one point as a 'has been' town. Ten years ago, a resurgence started. It now has a Lowe's Distribution Center, Entek (manufacturing battery separators), several other manufacturing businesses, a five-star hotel called The Boulder Falls Inn and a Western University Medical (Osteopathic) School with 400 students. It's the first new medical school in Oregon in over 100 years. The county's junior college offers an advanced automotive training program in Lebanon and Adam says, "It seems like there are always new areas of growth and excitement happening here." Adam and Kelsie moved to Lebanon six years ago and have worked on civic committees to keep the town moving forward. "It's our town and we're proud to be here," Adam says.

Adam has chaired the Lebanon Health Careers Ladder and has donated money enough to the medical school and its programs that he has his own study room where Adam has his floss, tooth brushes and other marketing materials available for the students. He was on Lebanon's visioning committee and the result was a solid plan to revitalize the downtown. He also was on the Lebanon city budget committee and has been involved with the local government. He has been involved with the Lebanon Downtown Association, voted Junior First Citizen in Lebanon and his business was voted Small Business of the Year. Adam says in the last 10 years, Lebanon is "rocking."

Adam has five on his dental team and two are a married couple. His hygienist MaryAnn is married to his assistant, Ted and amazingly enough they get along well and take great care of people. His team lives the vision and make many decisions following Adam's vision. At their morning meeting, they orally recite their office purpose, lending voice to their commitments to their guests.

They recently changed from three days of eight hours to four days of six hours each. It is the same number of weekly hours, just a different configuration for more family time every day. They work the equivalent of 114 days a year with 13 weeks off. In their 12 cycles, they are goaling at $95K in 9.5 days.

Adam is accomplished at wisdom teeth, endo, implants (UoP had an extensive implant course), same day crowns and dentures. He has completed seven of the nine courses in the Kois continuum. Dr. Kirkpatrick has a minimal sedation certification now and he wants to become IV certified as he presently uses a traveling dentist who does his IV sedation. He feels with IV training he would be using it weekly rather than once a quarter. His patients love that Adam does not refer out very often.

He wants to learn to treat sleep apnea. He values the work that he does for people and his commitment is for his treatment to withstand the test of time.

Adam's wife, Kelsie was a CPA who worked in SF during Adam's dental school. She is mom to three little ones and has started to home school their children. Professionally, Kelsie is an incredibly talented and organized person and, as Adam's partner, gained a great deal of insight to both how dentists think and feel as well as how dental businesses run. This perfect storm led to her starting her own dental bookkeeping business, serving dental clients all over the United States. Adam is grateful for the fact that she takes care of so many of the things that he really doesn't enjoy doing so his energy is directed to the things that he does enjoy. Now, with her business well established and three little ones at home to take care of, she has teamed up with other financial professionals to allow her to spend more time and energy at home.

Adam is grateful for getting to practice dentistry with such advanced technology, "Where people are so much more comfortable and we can do unmatched quality." He is happy that he gets to live in a great town and he adores time he gets to spend with his family. "Without the Blatchford team," he writes, "none of this would be possible. Thank you so much for helping me achieve my dreams!"

www.kirkpatricksmiles.com

Blatchford Game Plan: Two Hours to the Future

Drs. Fernandes and Kirkpatrick epitomize the necessary change from dental technician to manager and then the struggle to really lead. You can taste their struggle and see their emergence as strong winners who know what they want. Reading *E-Myth Revisited* by Michael Gerber demonstrates many of us in dentistry are stuck at the technician level and are frustrated. Life can be different.

We have all made a choice to be in dentistry. For many of us, the fulfillment of our days is in the intricacies of developing the perfect treatment plan, the challenge of creating a dazzling smile, the reward of the radiant result.

These are the technical skills at which some dentists excel. This is what dentists love to do. That is why the decision was initially made to become a dentist. In dental school the techniques and skills were taught so that upon graduation, the new dentist could immediately begin helping mouths to become healthy and smiles to be beautiful. Upon graduation, many thought that their skills and a sign on the door would be enough to gain patients. For many, while their technical dental skills were excellent, their ability to run a dental practice would become a continual struggle.

Statistics show that 95% of businesses fail when technical skills alone are relied upon. In this era, good, or even outstanding, technical skills are not enough to ensure success.

Merely fixing teeth for 40 hours a week will give a dentist a slim chance at financial success and a rewarding life.

This grim statistic is balanced by a simple solution. Choose to do treatment 28 hours a week and spend an additional four hours per week on management. Staffing, budgeting, brainstorming and training with the team, scheduling for profitability and associated factors, all play a vital role in the success and profitability of the practice. These four hours are well spent as they can actually double the gross of the practice!

The Four Hours

In these four hours the doctor performs as a manager. The time is spent on the needs of the practice—not the patients. As a manager, the finances would be reviewed, the profit and loss statements and monitors checked—what aspect of the practice is doing well, where is help needed? Team meetings would be prepared, who's in charge of the meeting, what is the topic, what areas are challenging and need addressing, what areas are doing exceptional and need recognition? Analysis of the marketing would be done, is it effective, are targeted patients being reached, does it need updating?

With good management, these four hours a week can result in an incredible increase in the annual gross. It can double! For example, "Dr. Technical" works 40 hours a week for a year doing the dentistry he loves to do. He grosses $125,000 that year. The doctor next door, "Dr. Manager" adds another four hours a week in efficiently managing the practice plus 28 with patients. This doctor is aware of his finances and is proactive with their information. The staff is competent and proficient. They work well as a team offering excellent dentistry. The patients are scheduled profitably. The marketing is successful and up to date.

"Dr. Manager" earned $250,000 working 32 hours. These four hours doubled the annual gross.

"Dr. Manager" is feeling pretty good! His additional four hours have really made a difference. Not only did he make more money, he has a competent staff that schedules well, leaving him time to spend with his family. Life is good. But with a mere two additional hours per week, it could be even better.

The Two Hours

"Dr. Leadership" spends an additional two hours as CEO in the practice. He is a visionary who looks into the future and develops the dream. He is the leader. It is his vision that inspires the team. He communicates it clearly so that all can see it, communicates it enthusiastically so that all believe in it, communicates it with such inspiration that all want to share in it.

The CEO is the master of the future. These two hours bestow the possibility of earning substantially more. What is the goal? 500K? A million? 3 Million? More? The clarity of the vision and the ability to communicate it well are the key to attainment.

A leader's job is providing the vision. That can be a difficult task in dentistry as most dentists are more comfortable in "left-brain" activities. Most gravitate to the technical, the "how-to" of things. To develop a vision, the right side of the brain needs to be fired up. A CEO focuses on the future. To facilitate future focus a leader answers these questions as if it was now 10 years into the future:

- Where are you? What city? Where is your practice? What is its atmosphere? What equipment is being used?

- How many days a week are you working? Which days? How many hours?

- What is your net income?

- What is your mix of treatment?

- What is your overhead?

- How many staff do you have? What are they like?

- Who are your patients?

- What type of marketing do you do?

- What are you "known as"?

The answers to these types of questions define the vision. The more detailed the vision, the more clearly it is communicated, the more it is shared with enthusiasm, the greater the possibilities of attainment. The team is completely enrolled in the vision. That is leadership. That is what propels the "Dr. Leaderships" to where they are.

Who do you choose to be? Take action in the development of your dream. Hold yourself accountable for the future and it will be the future you envision.

Bill Blatchford, DDS

From the Blatchford Play Book: Team Pitfalls

- ► Having the wrong team and not recognizing it
- ► Having a micro-manager as the leader belittles team and no one wants or needs to step up
- ► Failing to communicate the vision or hold it as your own
- ► Subgrouping or gossiping about other team members, doctor or patients
- ► Failure to form a real team
- ► Becoming stuck in tasks by losing sight of the bigger picture
- ► Allowing an attitude of mediocrity to prevail rather than one of winning
- ► Forgetting who we are serving
- ► Not having an effective bonus system
- ► Failure to learn and apply new technical, sales and marketing skills
- ► Not having regular morning meetings or weekly staff meetings
- ► Working overtime and blaming it on someone else
- ► Continually running late in hygiene and doctor schedule will decrease new patient flow
- ► Allowing personal issues to pervade the practice
- ► Allowing non-professional behavior to be the practice norm
- ► Superstars are generally not great team players

8

MENTORS

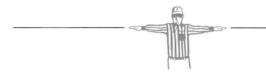

Drs. Dennis and Marie Stiles

This is a true family of dentists. Marie and Dennis are both children of dentists, their son is in an oral surgery residency at Jackson Memorial Hospital and they have three nieces who have chosen dentistry as their professions. Marie's two brothers are dentists and Dennis' sister is a hygienist. They both teach on Fridays at the University of Maryland and are committed to continuing to promote the advantages of private practice with solid skills.

In Gaithersburg, Maryland, 25 miles north of Washington DC, they share a general dental practice. Marie is certified in IV sedation and Invisalign plus practicing pedo and restorative dentistry. Dennis enjoys restoring implants, sleep apnea and cosmetics. Dennis teaches at the GPR Program at U. of Maryland where there are students from Saudi Arabia, Kuwait, Egypt and South America as a high demand to become credentialed. Some students are two years, some are three and four years. Many are foreign with families paying graduate tuition.

Both have trained at the LD Pankey Institute. "Bill helped us implement the clinical training from the Institute by teaching us patient case presentation skills, leadership and office team organization for our relationship based practice." Dennis was just elected to serve a three-year term on the LD Pankey Institute Board of directors.

Dennis and Marie have been Blatchford clients for over eight years. They were introduced to Blatchford by a former hygienist, now a seasoned enroller for Blatchford. They knew they needed a push. Now, they see this time as their transition into their second half of practice life. They feel they have new energy and focus. They are pleasantly finding with strong systems and a united doctor vision, there is more fun and more time.

They now take a solid eight weeks off. They know time away creates energy to be at their best. We want to avoid burnout as when attitude falters, diagnosis and focus drops. Dennis and Marie know team composition can fluctuate. Right now, their team has about two years experience together. Dennis and Marie brought them to a Blatchford seminar and continue to work on cross-training, sales conversations, vision. Team is each bonusing between $800 and $1100 every month.

The Stiles have frequently had a student intern with the intent of showing them the inside of dentistry. These are usually pre-dental students in college and there is a selection process. They find out about the office through a local pre-dental club at their college.

Dennis and Marie say they will probably never retire. They like Blatchford's Retire As You Go and may move to patient contact for three weeks and look to time away. They have a home on Singer Island near Palm Beach, FL. Both enjoy the generations and patient contact. They have a lot of TLC with their patients.

They have three children, spread out all over the country. The daughter lives the closest, soon to be married and living in Annapolis, Maryland. She is the director of social media at a large company and keeps them current on the newest trends in social media marketing. The middle child, the oldest son, is currently an oral surgery resident in Miami, Florida, and the youngest son lives in Los Angeles where he works in the movie/tv/entertainment industry. "Thanks to Blatchford, we have ample time to visit our children and have them show us around their beautiful cities."

Marie spent every summer from the age of 13 working in her father's practice until dental school. There was a sense of financial confidence growing up, but more importantly what she observed was an environment in her dad's practice of compassion and respect. Through his example, her father showed her how to treat each patient with dignity and patience—and her father's patients treated him with respect and admiration in return. Dennis' father was also beloved by his patients.

Dennis and Marie met in their first year of dental school in gross anatomy. Dennis was showing off all of his knowledge of anatomy from his experience as a teaching assistant in college. They started as study partners then Dennis asked Marie out in November of 1982. They were married the summer after junior year of dental school and graduated from Georgetown in the spring of 1986.

The one thing both Dennis and Marie would recommend to the newly minted dentist is not to fear the opportunities to create a private care relationship-based practice. With proper coaching and a team of advisors, it is still very realistic to buy a practice and develop a brand that is fee for service and relationship based. It is also an excellent way to confidently pay back student debt.

Currently, thy are lucky enough to make about four trips per year to Florida for extended stays of about 10 days each. They hope to increase that each year, at least Marie hopes to spend more of the winter there! Dennis and Marie do not have Florida licenses yet. They may consider this in the future.

They have had some amazing trips, most with and some without our children, including trips to Hawaii, Mexico, Europe, an Alaskan cruise, and most recently an African safari and a visit to South Africa's wine region. All three of their children spent a semester abroad; one in London, one is Spain, and one in Australia. All have a love of traveling!

www.stilesdentistry.com

Blatchford Game Plan: There Is No Final Answer

Bright, curious, knowledge seekers, Drs. Dennis and Marie Stiles push themselves to learn more and apply new knowledge from continuing education courses. Constantly reading and evaluating, they are a wealth of thoughts and ideas to implement into dentistry. For the Stileses there is no final answer.

Many dentists are comfortable with the status quo by clinging to traditional methods and ways of thinking, rather than seeking the possibility of a better result. Change is a challenge. We stay with the answers we know, rather than risking something new.

In *Who Moved My Cheese?*, Dr. Spencer Johnson shares some eagerly look for cheese in another spot, some reluctantly find cheese in another station and others would rather die when the cheese is not in the same spot.

In dentistry, the cheese has moved. New answers are available technically, in sales conversations and in marketing opportunities. Are you content or is there more "cheese" to be learned?

The top 10% of dentists know there can be no final answer. Approach the successful practice of dentistry as a constant work in progress. Are you part of the dental revolution or are you in the stands watching?

The most exciting aspect of the dental revolution is the technical advances. With bonded dentistry, new materials and techniques, you and your laboratory are able to deliver beauty, comfort and longevity. Your patients want to look good, feel good and last a long time.

The insurance game is another area where Doctors can feel trapped yet reluctant to change. Dentists, staff and patients have become willing partners for 40 years. We have allowed insurance companies to market and sell dentistry in your office. If your desire is to be insurance free, you must create a new image and become very skilled in sales and listening.

Dentists do have a clear choice to continue the same or become insurance free, mentally and financially. With any change, create a plan towards insurance freedom. Do the math, work with your staff on scripting and speak with every patient who is involved, sharing the benefits. Forever being a dental insurance provider is not necessarily the final answer.

Blatchford Coaching has led the way to another change—our patients do not NEED our services. Virtually everything we do is a choice. This coaching is different than taught and shakes the very core of insurance paradigms. When the NEED paradigm is resolved in dentists' minds, it creates the opportunity to help patients develop dreams of good-looking smiles. There is no final answer here, either, for as the marketplace changes, the skills and attitudes in dentistry will shift, too.

Learning sales skills is a real change. Stop the pressure sales of talking patients into fixing things. Learn to ask questions about their long term goals. Take a dental sales course like Blatchford Coaching. Have right-brained conversations. Start a sales library. There is definitely no final answer in the sales arena for just when you think you have it, the marketplace changes and dentistry takes a different position of choice.

In dental marketing, there is no final answer. Many dentists are slow to embrace the importance of marketing. The public recognizes dentistry is a choice and not a NEEDED service. Since dentistry is a choice, develop a niche and be the leader. Create a long-range plan, based on your personal vision and values and seek expert advice to position yourself as the expert in your area. Marketing in dentistry will never have a final answer as it is fluid and dynamic. Lead the marketplace, for if you wait for every answer, it is too late.

You do not have the final answer if your overhead is near 75% or higher. High overhead is a choice. The bigger, busier model of trying to be "everything to everyone" results in a higher overhead. It takes more staff for smaller procedures on many patients. Change the mix of treatment being offered to more optional services. Offer choices, not just the "patch-type" dentistry. Resign from the Crown of Year Club where the staff percentage is near 30% and the lab is under 10%. A lower overhead percentage means acquiring new skills and attitude.

Think of the passion in serving patients with beautiful, optional smiles. There is no final answer. Revisit your reasons for entering dentistry. Is there satisfaction in keeping things the same or is there a real possibility for you to take some risk, learn new skills and rekindle the excitement you first felt in being a dentist? The skills, knowledge and coaching are available to you. Take a chance. Give it your best.

Bill Blatchford, DDS

From the Blatchford Play Book: Coaching the Team

Drs. Dennis and Marie Stiles are both strong people persons, very introspective and sensitive. They are good listeners which is a fine quality for coaching a team to results.

► Discover your vision

► Write your vision

► Communicate your vision to your team

► Never compromise your vision

► Keep your eye on the ball

► There are no favorites on your team. Communicate equally

► Praise often, in public and with specifics

► Communicate what you stand for and what you don't stand for

► Don't allow anything less than 100% from yourself or your team members

► Don't let a bad apple spoil the team. Throw out the bad apple

► Constructive criticism is done privately, timely and with specific requests for change

► Make the hard decisions

► Be the leader who walks the talk; team expectations of conduct are the same for you, the leader

► Do not have any business dealings or loans with your team members

► Dress appropriately, speak well and carry a positive attitude at all times

► You must have respect. People do not have to like you but respect is an absolute

► Allow staff to grab responsibility and run with it

► Avoid "micro-managing" like the plague. Hire great staff and let them be accountable when it works and when it doesn't.

A World War II story showed President Franklin Roosevelt visiting an aircraft manufacturing plant and boosting morale. The first worker, when asked what he was doing, replied, "Placing screws in the wing." The second worker when asked, replied, "I am cutting the sheet metal for the tail gunner section." The third worker when asked, replied, "I am preserving our freedoms." Moral of the story: coach to the bigger picture. The details don't matter.

9

TEETH TOMORROW

Drs. Claudia Patch and Michael Tischler

Dr. Claudia Patch and Dr. Michael Tischler now own separate practices in the same building, each focusing on dentistry of their passion.

Claudia was truly inspired by *Playing Your A Game*. "I am so pleased to be part of the Blatchford 2.0 Book featuring young women who are working toward a better life balance of motherhood, professional dentistry and business leadership. I love that I was asked to help other women who want to have it all, " says Dr. Patch.

Claudia is the leader and owner of Tischler and Patch Dental, a restorative practice in Woodstock, NY (pop. 5800). The implant and surgical practice is owned by Dr. Michael Tischler, a friend and mentor to Claudia for nearly seven years. Together, Michael and Claudia helped to put into place a very successful full arch implant solution utilizing the Prettau implant bridge, called "Teeth Tomorrow," at their practice. Claudia lectures with Michael and teaches the prosthetic components of this implant solution.

Claudia was previously working as Michael's associate along with two part-time and one full-time associates and the practice was producing $6M. Now, as two separate entities under one beautiful roof, each portion is doing very well with renewed focus, efficiency and productivity.

Claudia has two children, Scarlett age three and Logan age one. Her husband is a NY police officer serving for the City of NY Department of Environmental Protection and Counter Terrorism (guarding the city's water sources). Claudia and her husband met in high school and he has always been an unwavering source of support for Claudia.

Claudia became interested in dentistry early as she had an admirable female orthodontist who touted the field of dentistry for its ability to provide tremendous personal satisfaction and the rewards of patient care while allowing for balance with one's personal life. Dr. Patch graduated from UCONN in 2009 and then did a one-year AEGD at the VA. Claudia and Michael met while Claudia was still in residency and Michael waited six months for Claudia to finish before she became an associate at their very busy practice. In the time Claudia was an associate, practice production grew by millions.

Though she had always wanted to be an entrepreneur, the practice was all consuming. Even as an associate, Claudia felt if she wasn't at the office, it would all fall apart. Days were long and intense. Claudia was practicing five days per week with two weeks vacation and she felt that even if she worked Saturdays and Sundays, she couldn't get it all done. She definitely was on the hamster wheel and felt she couldn't be the outstanding provider she aspired to be. Alone, Claudia was producing $1.4M but the work/life balance her childhood orthodontist had spoken of seemed like a distant dream..

When Michael approached Claudia about buying the entire practice while on maternity leave, Claudia was devastated to have to decline. Overhead was a beast and Claudia witnessed the stress this brought Michael on a daily basis. Claudia felt there was no way that she could manage the demands of the practice with a toddler and infant at home. With Blatchford's help, Bill and Michael made a proposition to split the practice into a surgical practice owned by Michael and a general dental practice owned by Claudia while systematically putting the Blatchford principles into place to control overhead. It was the perfect solution! Claudia was all-in and hasn't looked back.

With the best of the original team members behind her and Christina as her coach, Claudia felt like she was able to start her practice while flying in the jet stream. Under Claudia's leadership, the team kicked into action immediately. "I felt like I had an instruction manual for success and all I had to do was follow it," Claudia said. "Even though I have a large business loan to repay, I haven't felt this little stress in years."

When Claudia became an owner, she expected that the Blatchford systems would take time to show results. The results, however, exceeded her expectations. With her smaller team of one full-time (four days per week) associate, one part-time (one day per week) associate and 2.75 hygienists, production exceeded $580,000 in the first two months of practice. Of course, this was all while working one less day per week than before and in spite of taking an 11-day vacation during this period. "The team is getting huge bonuses and I couldn't be happier to write those checks. I am so proud of them," says Claudia.

Dr. Patch feels she is so fortunate and grateful, she cannot believe the results have been so rapid. The Patch team has only had one of the two Blatchford seminars. They are on fire!

Claudia is so excited, she told the team that when they are producing $3.5M, she will take them all on a Caribbean cruise. Wow!

claudia@tischlerdent.com

Dr. Michael Tischler

This talented dentist is first a husband of 26 years, a father of two nearly adult girls and a passionate implant dentist. It was his practice in Woodstock which he grew to a $6M with five dentists and 25 staff members.

Now, Dr. Tischler's practice is all surgery and implants. He is passionate about implants and teaching. Before Blatchford's Coaching and dividing the practice, he had worked five days a week with three weeks vacation for 25 years. One of the dentists was his 83-year-old father who continued to love dentistry. Michael was the responsible dentist for this whole practice. He was ready to relinquish some of the leadership.

This very successful practice had reached a point of total frustration for the owner. He loves implants and surgery. All the other procedures, including hygiene checks had lost the thrill for Dr. Tischler. When Bill offered the opportunity to sell the restorative, prosthodontic and hygiene as a separate unit and in the same building, Michael could see the possibilities as both practices are being coached by Blatchford. There is more time and greater net for both doctors.

Now, Dr. Tischler's passion is evident. He believes in what he is doing, lives it and loves it. He loves to do full arch surgery. To that end, his goal is $60K a day three days a week. It takes him two hours for upper and lower which equals a morning. He does not make his goal every day but it is a realistic vision and he and his team are trending towards it.

Dr. Tischler feels setting goals for him will create a balance between career and health. He has always worked with his team in training and rewards. He wants to make his team the very best.

Michael is a like a Renaissance man with many talents and interests. He loves what he does and wants to share it with others with a program called Teeth Tomorrow which has 230 more franchises available for dentists to deliver the kind of dentistry being accomplished in Woodstock. By the end of 2017, 125 dentists will be delivering Teeth

Tomorrow and in 2018, there will be the full 250 Dentists. These are franchises with full-arch focus, training for Doctor and team, branding including web, print, television, support and mentorship. Michael passionately shares there is a need for this quality of dentistry everywhere. It is ubiquitous in America. According to the CDC, in NY state, 22% of those over 65 are completely edentulous. The average patients are between 50 and 60. Both Claudia and Michael are teachers and so enjoy the opportunity. Each franchise has 1.15M population base.

The Tischer Dental office is incredibly beautiful and Michael feels the office décor is part of marketing and setting a high standard. This facility is beautifully furnished, 12 treatment rooms along with a training center, lecture hall and lunch room for 50 people.

Dr. Tischler is also an artist and had a gallery in SoHo, now has design groups representing him. It is an unusual and very special HDR High Dynamic Range with printing on aluminum.

Michael also has Tischler Dental Lab which is blending his passion with several businesses. The Tischler Dental Lab is working with Teeth Tomorrow in offering the Prettau Bridge.

Michael feels life is like a painting, making good strokes and done well. He is quite amazed at the Blatchford result of dividing his practice into two very rewarding parts and he is very appreciative of having Dr. Claudia Patch in this fascinating dental relationship.

mt@tischlerdental.com

The reception area at Tischler Dental

Dr. Tischler lecturing on Teeth Tomorrow

Blatchford Game Plan:
"Spot On" Behavior Checklist

Drs. Patch and Tischler are passionate in working with their teams to offer the best. They market heavily and work with their teams to develop behavior consistent with the best choices. Tischler Dental teams do know how to serve well. They see the bigger picture and are branding themselves as different.

Positive thoughts, goals and talk make a real difference in the success of your practice. However, the only concrete evidence of positivity is demonstrated by doctor and staff action, behavior and results. Putting words into action is a choice. Walking your talk is a choice. Our behavior and results are a choice. Turning goals and lofty dreams into reality is a choice, a choice every minute of our day.

Our doctors call it "spot on" behavior. It is a moment to moment choice to play the game and play it well. In *Maximum Achievement*, Brian Tracy says "Everything counts, everything counts, everything counts." Knowing our behavior is a choice, how well do we choose every minute? What systems are in place in ensure our goals are met and exceeded? "Spot on" behavior is reaching down deep to accomplish your own maximum achievement.

"Spot on" behavior is avoiding sending in the mail an extensive health history to a new guest who will be entering our practice with a prophy. Rather, sit with the guest and complete a shorter health history together. It is time and commitment to make a new guest comfortable.

"Spot on" is having meaningful conversations with guests about their dental dreams. Rather than waiting until the appointment end, a choice in behavior is to ask questions, listen with intention and help your guest build their picture of their smile. The other choice in behavior is to be "too busy" and avoid the conversation completely.

"Spot on" behavior is utilizing a state sanctioned opportunity for hygienists to administer anesthesia. When a recare patient has a single filling diagnosed, scheduling a separate appointment is a time challenge for patient and practice. Instead, at the next hygiene cleaning, the hygienist can deliver the anesthesia and the doctor can complete the filling in the hygiene chair.

"Spot on" is discovering your guest's personal preferences for coffee, music, temperature or movies and delivering upon their arrival. Anticipation turns words into action and this earns loyalty from your patients.

"Spot on" behavior is the doctor answering and asking more questions, ultimately giving an estimate to the patient. Trust and loyalty is developed when the doctor completes the diagnosis and gives a fee. More cases are still pending or lost when a transfer of responsibilities occurs in midstream. Completing the job is a choice in behavior. When there is a definite "yes" to treatment and the fee is given, the financial expert in your practice can do the logistics of money.

"Spot on" is an assistant leading his/her room by being totally prepared and orally completing a laminated checklist. It is an assistant running the room on time. In a diagnosis of crowns and fillings, it is an assistant who has the doctor complete the fillings first, knowing the doctor will always complete the crown. It is an assistant who is conscious of patient's time and practice profitability to complete the scheduled work on time.

"Spot on" behavior is seeing the big picture of scheduling in blocks so the doctor has minimal interruptions. It is scheduling hygiene with periodontal patients during the doctor's production blocks. It is communicating with team to meet goal as one.

"Spot on" is seeing every guest as a person and not as a set of teeth dropped off at your office. If you have a picture in your mind of what you would like this person to look like, your own agenda will trip you every time. "Spot on" is acknowledging your guest as a full person with likes and dislikes. Developing their dreams, not yours, will give you the results at which you are goaling.

"Spot on" is seeing yourself as an innovator, working and thinking about the patient's impressions. Malcolm Gladwell, in his book *blink*, confirms people make up their mind about something in seconds. Therefore, "spot on" is thinking on your feet as well as having systems in place to demonstrate you are worth it.

"Spot on" behavior results from systems of communication, skill-building, scheduling, and most of all a leader who sets the direction which motivates a team of people who see the doctor's vision as their own.

Bill Blatchford, DDS

From Blatchford Play Book: Extra Effort

Drs. Tischler and Patch are helping dentists create a new higher standard of care. They are both passionate in their lessons. It does take extra effort to achieve the result of which you dream.

- ► Reach down deep for that something extra
- ► Want it bad enough
- ► Learn to play with a relaxed concentration
- ► I want my team and I to make that second effort
- ► We have more potential than we realize. Use it.
- ► A winning team has dedication, they will not accept defeat; they will make that extra effort
- ► You need to have a motive which has extraordinary appeal
- ► Set a goal to be the very best and then work every waking hour of each day trying to achieve that goal
- ► Condition yourself to master case presentation by reading a book on sales or marketing every week.
- ► Practice with a video camera. Watch it yourself and eliminate movements or expressions you do not like or are distracting
- ► Avoid the word NEED in conversations with your guests
- ► Connect on some level with everyone
- ► Don't be overly concerned about what other dentists think
- ► Always dress the part

10

RETIRING IN TEN YEARS

Dr. Dale Schisler

Eleven years ago Dr. Schisler was questioning if he could continue in dentistry at the pace his practice required. He was 60 and had 17 people working with him, producing $650K. That February, he and his wife took no salary but paid all other bills. He knew he needed a real change. He was looking for a way out.

Dale attended a Blatchford seminar, More Profits, More Time Off with Dr. Bill Blatchford. Twenty minutes into the lecture, Dale chose 'yes,' went to the back of the room and asked how he could sign up. He so related to the Blatchford philosophy and Bill, that Dale jumped on it.

After just one Blatchford year, the team of seven produced $1.2M because, Dale says, the team started selling both the practice and dentistry.

He feels Blatchford helped create a new culture of success. He is the leader and sets the vision. The team carries him. 80% of their patients come from referrals and the team is constantly promoting the practice wherever they are.

His assistant has been with him 42 years and others, 35 and 25 years. Dale loves the Blatchford bonus system. The team will go the extra mile as they like the monetary reward they earn and have adopted an attitude of ownership. They have the spirit to make profitability happen which means more time off with pay.

Today his team knows they need to produce $150K in a 15-day cycle. An ideal morning would be 3-4 patients and inserts in the afternoon. He does a lot of multiple units. He does not have a cone beam as the Royal Dental College of Ontario regulates their purchase, so he uses close-by radiologists. He also has a denturist who pays rent when there.

Now, at 71, and in good physical shape, he has told his inquiring patients for years, "Yes, I will retire in ten years." Dr. Schisler says that reply allows him to acknowledge their kind inquiry and also allows him always, ten more years.

He embodies the Blatchford concept of Retire As You Go. Dale says Bill explained to him, "When you sell your practice, it will be about one year's net to you. You have a good thing going, Dale. Eliminate the treatments you are not in love with and add those which intrigue you. Keep practicing for ten years and enjoy the net of ten or more years."

Now taking ten weeks off a year, Dale has a personal trainer, keeps his weight under control, is a cross country jogger and when we talked on the phone, he was fly fishing on the bank of the Grand River, enjoying life. He feels his hobbies require him to be in good shape and that feeling of good health carries over to dentistry.

Dale was the first in his family to go to college. His father was a steel worker and his parents' dream was for the children to be educated. They were very proud for Dale to become a dentist. Of the 20 cousins, only four went to college. He and Marg, who have been married for 49 years, have contributed to the 10 grandkids' (ranging from 6 to 17 years) college funds and helped the children with down payments for homes.

At the time of frustration, Dale had two associates and a 25-year partner. He feels the partnership was one of the worst decisions he ever made. His feeling about partnerships is so strong, he advises any dentist who is even considering a partnership to call him and he will talk you out of it. He knows he is unemployable working for anyone.

Dale and team are the draw in a shopping mall. They are very visible and because it is a six-day mall, they need to be open those hours.

Dale works three days in the summer and he leaves at 3 pm.

He and his wife Marg will celebrate their 50th wedding anniversary in 2017. They have three children and 10 grandchildren who all live within driving distance. Dale said the best vacation was taking the whole group of 18 on a Disney cruise. He confesses he was a 'pirate sensation.' This year, they are renting a home in Florida for two winter months. Marg has been an integral part of Dale's success as she was the patient services confidant and mother hen.

As Dale shared in his Blatchford introduction "Peak Performance" he confessed, he was sleeping with a teammate. Seminar participants did not know how to react. Then he said, it was Marg who embraced the Blatchford Solution and supported Dale every step along the way, LOL.

Through Crown Council, Dale has done ten volunteer trips to the Dominican Republic cane fields with a mobile dental unit. He remembers one local patient asking him about the rumor that Canadians actually feed food to their dogs.

Dale can speak French, so can communicate with Haitians, who are badly neglected in the Dominican. He feels volunteering changes your life.

Five years ago, the team pushed him to learn to place implants. He studied with Carl Misch and also took a residency at the University of Toronto which was 20 three-day weekends with live patients. Dale enjoys implants and his team was right to push him.

Dale is in a good financial position with no debt so he is not counting on the sale of his practice for his retirement. He loves what he is doing and "will probably retire in 10 years." We wish him well.

www.hopedaledentalcare.com

Pirates extraordinaire, Dale and Marg

Blatchford Game Plan: The Legacy of Sgt. Schultz

In these changing times, people are looking for solid relationships and comfort close to home. Especially, in dentistry, your patients need to feel they know you and can trust you. In dental sales, we have long held the idea that building patient trust is explaining and educating the patient on the technical aspects of treatment. Great acceptance does not result.

Sergeant Schultz on the old comedy, "Hogan's Heroes" had the real attitude for successful dental sales in these changing times. His most often response in a fabulous German accent, was, "I know nothing." In successful dental sales, we need to have our minds be like a blank canvas ready for the patient to paint the picture. We must assume the attitude that "I know nothing" about this person. I am here to learn.

If you begin the sales process (the time before the patient says "yes") with your answer for them without involving the patient's desires, we miss the whole point of sales. The sales process is the emotional right-brained portion where we ASK about dreams, desires, benefits, results, not how fabulous our preconceived answer will be for them.

A dentist is so technically trained, we inhibit the sale process. Our mind is constantly designing our idea for a perfect smile for the new patient, the grocery clerk, the waiter or our karate instructor. However, in the sales process, we trip over our own feet when we already have a picture in mind for our patient.

Lou Holtz said, "I never learn anything talking. I only learn when I ask questions." Imagine if another football great, Vince Lombardi was a new guest in your office. Immediately you see your ideas of how to change the dyastima, the spacing and flat yellow teeth. Without finding what Mr. Lombardi wants, you begin describing what you would do for him. In telling him about your plan for his spacing and dyastima, he replies (with some indignation) "What do you mean, change my smile? My smile is a Lombardi smile. It is the same as my father and grandfather. No way." On a scale of one to ten, how are you doing on building relationship and trust?

The Boat Sales Person of the Year explained his success by saying, "When I see an inquiring couple, I never begin with a boat in mind." Imagine a dentist as a realtor showing homes before finding the dreams and desires of the client. The dentist would point to the features the dentist sees, like the lovely flowering cherry tree or the beautiful outdoor patio for summer dining. By asking more questions, deeper questions, the dental-realtor could have discovered the potential home buyer has severe allergies to trees and bees. The sale is blown.

For a successful sale, the technically trained must clear their mind. "I know nothing" becomes your mantra. Our job is to help the patient uncover THEIR agenda. Develop a trusting relationship by staying out of the "tooth talk" while you develop a friend.

If you keep asking questions, the patient will paint a picture for you. Their answers will sound like looking good, younger, whiter, straighter, more even smile, looking better, lasting a long time and feeling better about their smile. Ask them to expand on these thoughts. Have them select an after picture to help them visualize their dream smile. Have them describe it, sharing advantages if they owned that smile.

Because you began the conversation with the Sgt. Schultz's attitude of "I know nothing," you allow the patient to paint their own picture. They can see it, it is their idea and they will defend their idea. They will resist your agenda. You put unwanted pressure on them to accept what you had in mind.

Create the opportunity for your new friend to dream into the future about their smile. Start with "I know nothing" and your patient will fill your brain with more and better ideas than you ever thought.

By beginning with "I know nothing," you can avoid the Ricky Ricardo line of "you have a lot of 'splaining to do."

Bill Blatchford, DDS

From the Blatchford Play Book: Keeping Score

Dr. Schisler and team are very conscious of numbers, time and efficiency. To achieve a balance, knowing the score is essential.

▶ Know your numbers and what they mean

▶ Know which numbers can change and how to change them

▶ Reward your team monthly with an easy to figure and understand bonus

▶ Let your team understand the bonus math so they can increase their "ownership"

▶ Hire "10's" on your team and be a "10" yourself

▶ Use Pareto's 80/20 Rule—the top 20% of your guests deliver 80% of your profits. Who are they? Find out and nurture them.

▶ 20% of America moves each year. In a practice with 1000 patients, 200 will probably move. In order to grow 10%, you will need to attract 300 new patients or 25 a month. Who is in charge?

▶ Have a daily goal for doctor and hygiene.

▶ Diagnose three times your daily goal

▶ Know your overhead per hour and schedule to exceed it every hour

▶ Create a game plan when numbers are not met. Who is the source, what is the plan?

▶ Know your percentage of lab. National average is 8%. Are you above or below? What does that mean?

▶ Create a system to celebrate when numbers are met

▶ Team members know the score at all times

▶ "I do not know" is unacceptable. Be curious about the score.

▶ If you are not asking questions, it could seem you do not care about the score.

11

THE TEAM

All doctors have strongly indicated that excellent team players are a must. Doctors have shared their agonizing over staff who appear to be on a different path.

- Should I train them better?
- What if I lose the best team member I have?

Doctors rely on great staff to form a team and get the job done. Several team members volunteered their ideas on how they Bring their 'A' Game.

Dr. Christina Blatchford
Amanda Nash, Dental Assistant

How did we get started with Cerec? I remember the day I got a text message from Dr. Blatchford saying, "I bought a Cerec!" I had barely just found out the day before that she was going to a Cerec Accept class. The thought that was going through my head at the time was, yes! Bring on this new adventure! I was excited to see what kind of impact this would have on our dental practice. I knew that Dr. Blatchford and I were already a great team, and we would make the Cerec experience excellent. We received our Cerec computer, milling unit (which we fondly call "Millie"), and oven in March 2015. We immediately hit the ground running. Together, we have attended five classes for Cerec. In the year and a half since we first started Cerec we have learned so much.

It has had a very positive effect on our practice and in the lives of our patients. It usually starts with our hygienists, who present the treatment plan for the crown/crowns. Most of our patients that get a Cerec crown cannot believe that they get their permanent crown all in one visit. Patients have said things to me like, "There's no more goo?", "I can't believe the technology!", "Are you making my crown right now?", "It looks just like a tooth!", "It is amazing that you are making my crown right in front of me!", "It's like a 3D printer for my tooth". Many of our patients have expressed to me that they love that it only takes one appointment, they only have to be numb once, and it saves them the hassle of taking more time off work. Our patient acceptance of Cerec has been wonderful. I believe that is largely in part to the positive attitude of our team and the way we work together to give our patients the best experience.

Not only has Cerec had a positive impact on our patients and our practice, but it has also has a positive impact on me as well. I have had the opportunity to do much of the work with Cerec. From scanning digital impressions, to designing the crown, and staining/glazing them. I feel fortunate that I work with a dentist that has confidence in my abilities and has let me take the reins with Cerec. Not all dentists allow their dental assistants to utilize all their abilities, but Dr. Blatchford has done that with me. I think she realized my potential, before I even did. I believe our strong bond as a dentist/dental assistant team has allowed us to do more than I ever could have imagined.

Dr. Chris Campus
Nicki Mantuano

I have been in dentistry for 23 years. I had the privilege of joining Aggie Dental Center and Dr. Campus in December 2015. This was my first exposure to Blatchford Solutions.

Having a fee-for-service practice enables us to provide quality dental care without the limitations of dental insurance contracts. I coach our team to educate the patients in the benefits of coming to our practice. Part of this coaching involves using terms that make patients feel comfortable. For instance, when explaining benefits to a patient, "out-of-network" is replaced with "although we are not contracted with your insurance company, we file claims with them all the time." This is one of the reasons we are successful.

Block booking eliminates the stress of a hectic schedule. It's important to know what procedures are provided at the best time. It's also very important to have a team in place that is motivated enough to handle a change in that scheduling!

BAM has been one of the most exciting parts of Blatchford Solutions! It gives the team the opportunity to participate in the success of the practice. Our team has been eager to exceed our goals during each cycle. It's important to make sure everyone is working toward that goal. Although an office may have many different personalities, the ultimate purpose is to be rewarded financially while having the time off to enjoy life! If you find that an employee has any negativity or lack of enthusiasm, a Blatchford office may not be the place for them.

Ultimately, the success of the practice is based on collections. I've witnessed Dr. Campus gain treatment acceptance like no other! Doctors must be exceptionally confident in their ability to explain options to patients, while having the patient choose the best option given. We must place value on their decision to invest in their dental care. Having patients understand they must pay in full before treatment is provided, places value on the service we are providing. This is no different than people being willing to pay in full for a vacation they are booking. They are excited about this and we must present it in the same way.

Blatchford Solutions has been instrumental in the success of our practice. I look forward to many more years of guidance!

Nicki Mantuano

Dr. Leslie Gallon

We began as a well-run practice with a large staff of eight individuals. We worked well alongside each other but we were working separately. What was missing was a commitment to a clear and uniting vision. We honed it down to a tightly knit, talented team with a common focus, vision, and passion. And then it all began. . . .

Cross training and role-playing is where the rubber really hit the road for us. What felt uncomfortable at first has now become second nature (thanks to continual practice at monthly meetings). Using the Power Questions has transformed how we communicate with patients and each other. We notice daily that our patients are responding differently—they are more friendly and open. We have come to realize it is not our patients who have changed; it is us that have become more sincerely interested in them.

Blatchford has given us the confidence and tools so that anyone on the team can offer patients the best treatment and let them choose. We had to get over fear and become comfortable having patients say 'no'. It just means we have asked questions about what they want and given them the power to choose. We are always amazed how many of these 'no's' eventually become 'yes.' When patients know the possibilities, and know they are in control, minds often change on their own. We are all leaders who take the initiative to have conversations with patients about what their goals are, and take ownership for seeing opportunities and making things happen. Dr. Gallon says "when I can walk into a hygiene room and just say 'Yes, we can do that for you', as patient goals and treatment possibilities have already been discussed, that's Blatchford in action."

Learning to listen, not tell, to be interested rather than interesting, we have seen amazing things happen. Our lovely 80 year old patient confided in one of our team members how embarrassed she was feeling that her friends were always asking her if she had been eating blueberries as the edges of her teeth were so thin they appeared blue. We offered her the best treatment to give her a smile she could be proud to show off. Her daughter thought extracting the front teeth and making a removable partial denture was the better option. But although it was more of an investment than she initially planned, our patient said, "I want to save my teeth. I trust Dr. Gallon and I am going go with her recommendation". Seeing how her whole disposition changed, how bright and cheerful she was with her new smile, was a poignant reminder to always give someone the opportunity to choose the best treatment. It can be life changing.

Reviewing BAM daily and logging into Team IQ have been great motivators, as well as the inspiration from the books on Bill's must-read list. We aim to 'surprise and delight' daily. Whether its gathering together in the reception with a bottle of champagne wrapped in bright green tissue paper (our office color) to present to our latest smile makeover patient, or walking down the street in matching green scarves to congratulate a new office with an orchid, these small acts keep us and those around us smiling. We celebrate our accomplishments regularly. Seeing how far we have come, and hearing the achievements of other

Blatchford offices, keeps us excited to aim higher. Everyone looks forward to annual Blatchford conferences because we return energized from all the success stories and fresh ideas we want to incorporate for ourselves.

Instead of great individuals working in an office together, we now have a cohesive, motivated, and focused team that all share in the responsibilities and the rewards. We have a passion for what we do, the people we do it with, and the people we do it for. It's the team working together that makes the magic happen. And that's what was missing before and what we have now . . . magic.

The Gallon Team
Back row: Jessica, Ashley, Wonder Woman, Dr. Leslie Gallon.
Front row: Linda, Donna, Dr. Tamara Gallon

Dr. Steven Hatcher
Marsha Owens, Hygienist

Dr. Steven Hatcher and team members joining in why they like Blatchford Solutions:

Would you like to hear a no brainier?

Blatchford Solutions is the right solution. That is, if you would like professional success as well as personal success.

I thought I knew what a team was, but after being in this program for almost two years, I now know the true meaning. We are all willing to be coached and are coaches to each other. Now *that* is a team!

I have definitely become a more confident hygienist but more importantly a stronger person.

Topping that all off, I had nine weeks of time off in one year. How great is that? I highly recommend this program!!

Marsha Owens

Dr. Tracey Hughes
Shanda Hammond, RDH, BS

I have been with a best of the best, Blatchford doctor for the last five years, Dr. Tracey Hughes. I have learned so much about being part of an amazing team, and the benefits of working smarter to reach a goal. As a hygienist I have worked in many settings and never thought an office like this existed. I trust my team member's explicitly, feel like my voice is heard and valued, and feel willing to put in whatever is needed to make the day a success. I currently enjoy the benefits of working a 3.5 day week with a paid week of vacation every month. I have enjoyed the successes of over $10K in bonuses for the year. But the thing that matters most to me is the vision that the Blatchford program has given me. I plan and look forward to the time spent with my family, creating memories and doing things together. Just over the summer, I spent a week with my husband in Mexico celebrating our anniversary, took a road trip with all the kids to see family out of state and had a personal week to enjoy a conference with friends. This time to regroup, refocus and enjoy has brought a balance and passion to my life I didn't know was possible. Thank you Blatchford for the opportunity to thrive on this journey!

Dr. Steven Sirin
Mary Carol, Office Manager

Our practice started with the Blatchford group a month before my doctor decided to take over another practice. Joining two busy practices and moving ours to another building was a great undertaking since nothing was on a computer at the practice Dr. Sirin purchased. Being an office manager, this was a paperwork nightmare. We implemented all the ideas the Blatchford Group had suggested. The long hours were made tolerable by working the 15 days and then having time off. Our Team has reduced our days working by 41 and still increased our production by 79 percent. This personally gave me more time with my family which I have never had in the 37 years I have worked in a dental office. The cross training was a key to this giving all of our team time off. Even the books that were suggested to read like, *No Excuses* and *Integrity Selling* bolstered the ideas set forth by the Blatchford Group and helped in understanding what our new patients wanted from dentistry. This was a key in treatment planning. We have never had so much treatment accepted!

Nanci Granahan was such a BIG help personally with seeing what could be done to help our team make the transition go even smoother. Hygienists taking payments, getting our 4x4, AM and PM meetings on track. Cutting down even more time spent at the office. Nanci even fine-tuned our block scheduling to help with making our BAM goal, which we go over regularly.

I can't imagine what our team would have done with the transition if it wasn't for The Blatchford Group!

Dr. Chris Maestro
Cherie Janik, Hygienist

I joined the Maestro Dentistry in 1994. Being part of Dr. Maestro's team all these years has been such a privilege. It he helped me grow tremendously on both a personal and professional level. Working with such a great group of people and loving what you do and who you do it for is a true blessing. Since joining Blatchford in 2011, we have reached goals that at the beginning seemed insurmountable!! Our team had grown exponentially bringing so many advanced services to our patients along with putting systems into place to better serve them. Along with the benefits for our patients came the rewards of more time off to spend with our families as well as financial rewards which allowed me to purchase a new home.

In November of 2015, Dr. Maestro was involved in a very serious automobile accident while attending the Kois Center in Seattle, WA. This left him with injuries that prevented him from practicing for over six weeks. During this time, we all pulled together as the amazing team that we are and vowed we could and would get through this difficult time. I firmly believe our practice could not have survived this hardship without having the Blatchford training and systems in place. We overcame so much and proved we have the will and strength to achieve anything we put our minds to. We have rebounded and are continuing to set and reach new goals every day.

Dr. Chris Maestro
Erin McCollum, Patient Services Coordinator

Being the newest member of the Maestro Team, I can honestly say I have never experienced such loyalty, compassion and support from the people I work with almost every day. We are truly a team in every sense of the word. We all have a common goal and we give 100 percent to achieve that goal and more all while providing superior dental service and care to our patients. Accepting my position at Maestro Dentistry has given me security, and fulfillment. I knew from the first time I walked into the clean and inviting office that I would not only fit in but could see myself working there for a number of years. Then after getting to know Dr. Maestro and the rest of the team I knew I was in a good place. Dr. Maestro sets the bar high and I am happy to help this team reach goals and accomplish things that aren't easy.

Last November our team's strength was tested when our fearless leader was in a car accident. Never once was I worried. I knew that we needed to take care of our patients and come together to get the job done. Through it all our team demonstrated professionalism and hard work. We conquered a challenging time and won.

Working with Maestro Dentistry and being part of a Blatchford office has shown me that working together is the key to success. It is critical to find the right team. It has taught me that as human beings we can accomplish goals and dreams. I am fortunate to be a part of this remarkable team and will forever be grateful for finding such a wonderful group of people to work with.

Dr. Chris Maestro
Nancy Piché, CDA

I love being a part of the Maestro Dentistry team. From the day I first started, back in1998, I knew that I was not only working in a great place, but it seemed like the perfect place for me. Dr. Maestro has always made me feel like there is nothing I couldn't do if I put my mind to it. He always encourages me and everyone around him with his positive thinking and "can do" attitude. That came in very handy when he was badly injured last November in an automobile accident. With that same frame of mind, my three team members and I, took the reigns and were able to manage things at the office for a few weeks until THANKFULLY, Dr. Maestro was able to come back to work. We all felt blessed that he was recovering and that we were able to help keep things under control for him and for our patients while he was out. I believe that a lot of the faith, strength and confidence that we had and needed during that ordeal, came from being a Blatchford practice. I don't think any of us had any idea of our true potential or how much we could accomplish as a team before we started with Blatchford Solutions. With Blatchford's coaching, we were able to channel our enthusiasm, set goals, then reach and surpass them. Along with that, came great satisfaction and confidence, not to mention financial gains, more vacations and lots of happy patients. No wonder everyone smiles a lot at Maestro Dentistry!

Dr. Chris Maestro
Kara Peters, RDH

November 15, 2015 is a day that would change my life forever. When a crisis enters your life so unexpectedly you wonder how you will make it through. In the blink of an eye life as we knew it was rattled. Our leader was out of commission. I came to realize I could've lost my friends, my family, and my coworkers. But instead of this crisis bringing us down, it lifted us up, made us work harder and strive to pull through this stronger than before.

I knew when we started Blatchford Solutions that we were setting ourselves on a new path. But full appreciation for what we have become as a team changed when this crisis occurred. Blatchford Solutions has been a blessing to our practice. They have taught us too that being outside your comfort zone is where you achieve true success.

Blatchford Game Plan: No Telling In Selling

The winning teams are skilled in people conversations. They know the bigger picture and build trust with guests by asking questions and really listening. They know the 80/20 rule applies to successful sales in that you want your guest talking about their dreams and ideas 80% of the time.

Even quiet dentists and their staffs seem to talk too much during the sales process. Our four years of dental school and many continuing education courses have given us enough technical fuel to share your excitement and your plans for their mouth. You bore your patients and it is a fluke if someone says 'yes' to more than a broken tooth.

The sales portion of dentistry is when trust is built and relationships are formed. L.D. Pankey said "Know yourself, know your patient." Too often this is interpreted as know their 28 teeth. Become acquainted with your established patients and especially new guests in a different manner. Because you know nothing about the standards, values and dreams of this new guest, create different systems so you can develop their important trust.

When we talk technical dentistry during the sales process, you have not shown them any effort on your part to be interested in them and their dreams. Because we make decisions permanently, instantly and emotionally, when you start talking about your ideas for their smile without even knowing them, this is an affront to people and generally, they decide to turn you off. You can physically see these signs when they cross their arms, eyes looking for an escape and nod their head like they understand or care of what you are speaking.

Consider the value of trust and relationships. How do you develop and maintain personal friendships? The same factors are important to have a successful business. Time or the perception of time is an important factor. Caring is the other.

Creating time in a busy dental office is a matter of perception. If a new patient enters your office during a triple booked procedure with double hygiene going, where is the relaxed atmosphere we so desperately want? Always schedule new guests in the morning when you are block booked and the office really is relaxed and elegant. Be a great host to offer coffee, teas, juice in a real cup with a real napkin. Attractively framed after pictures adorn your walls and reading material is hardback books on area history, industry, humor or foods.

Show time and caring are important by inviting your new friend into a separate consult room to share their thoughts and information. Avoid handing them a clipboard, sitting alone and completing boring material. Make your forms short and do it with them. Make it interesting. A consult room should be a neutral site, one without an x-ray viewer, sample bridges which come apart or sharp instruments. If it was once the doctor's office, unload all the old magazines and dental items.

Your attitude and skill during these first ten minutes is to discover a new friend. Your job is to connect with them at some level. Interestingly, they do not care a lot about your family, experiences or thoughts. Focus on them. People think you are a terrific friend when you ask questions about them, their thoughts and ideas. Show you care by asking them questions and more questions. Do not come up with solutions at this time as it is too early. If they say, "I would like my teeth to look younger, my smile whiter"—an unfocused staff might say, "We could bleach them here or you could take it home." That is a solution too quick. Instead ask, "When did you first notice this?" "Tell me more about that?" "What have you tried so far?"

What you will find when you ask questions and show your caring, many people will warm to you and share much more then they had thought of initially. Someone who initially inquiries about whitening could have thoughts of never liking their smile, being laughed at in junior high, not having a lot of teenage fun all based on their perception that their teeth didn't look so great. All this still influences how they react to others. You will discover much about your new friend because they trust you.

The unskilled staff member above will possibly sell a bleach kit. The focused staff member who asked more and more questions with little or no dental tech talk may sell an unknown quantity of resulting satisfaction. Cut out the tech talk and ask THEM questions. It is a win/win.

Bill Blatchford, DDS

From the Blatchford Play Book: Team Rules

- ➤ Coach calls the game
- ➤ Be on time. Lombardi time is 15 minutes ahead of regular time
- ➤ Wear your uniform. Be proud, look your best and make your team look good
- ➤ Prepare yourself mentally to play the game
- ➤ Wear your game face proudly
- ➤ Play full out as you never know which play will make the difference
- ➤ Start your day with an effective morning huddle 15 minutes before your first play
- ➤ Be accountable for your actions. If the ball comes to you and you miss it, create a plan for that not to occur again. Accept responsibility and move on
- ➤ Do not hog the limelight. There are no stars on a winning team
- ➤ Make your teammates look good. Give them credit all the time
- ➤ Do not start derogatory or gossipy conversations about your coach, your team or the fans and do not listen to any team member who is the gossip. Instead, take them by the arm to share their "story" which the person who is the subject of their wrath. Bottom line, no trash-talking on the winning team.
- ➤ Treat other staff how you want to be treated
- ➤ Do not make anyone smaller than you
- ➤ If there is a problem, go to the source
- ➤ No whining. Instead, contribute positively and constructively. If you do not agree with something, think of a different plan and present it. Whining is a losing skill.
- ➤ Never admit to anyone you are tired, angry or bored
- ➤ Never carry a grudge. It is a waste of everyone's time
- ➤ Include everyone on your team in communication and training

- ► Holding "secrets" will destroy a team
- ► Learn something new every day. Read a sales or marketing book and apply it to your game.
- ► As a team, donate skills and time once a month to community service—walking dogs at the animal shelter, serving homeless meals, adopting a single-parent family, etc.
- ► Do volunteer dentistry in your community once a quarter. The whole team participates.
- ► Either you have your reasons or your results
- ► Be a team player 100%. During the game, you are focused. Home or relationship concerns are not part of your work conversations.
- ► Do not consume food in the work areas
- ► The winning players are those who think and know they can win.
- ► Learn the most important skill in sales—listening

12

A BALANCED LIFE

Dr. Ben Wang

Dr. Ben Wang practices general dentistry in downtown Portland, OR and is married to Dr. Liz Lee who offers pediatric dentistry in two locations east of downtown. They are raising three small children and seeking balance. Liz is actually a separate Blatchford client as they have separate practices. She, too, is a delight.

There are two main medical dental buildings in downtown Portland. Ben is not located in either one of the medical dental buildings but being in downtown Portland everything is walking distance. Ben was encouraged by his coach Dr. Christina Blatchford to find a practice to merge as downtown Portland is very competitive. The dental school is within two miles.

The retiring doctor initially did not want his patients to merge into another practice as he was concerned for his staff. A couple of offers failed and the doctor called Ben. Though the practice was equal size, he only hired one extra hygienist. The merger helped him to eliminate many PPO's. He started at $800K (working 208 days) with Blatchford and moved his practice to $1.2M and with the merger, it is $1.5M (working 144 days). It has helped with cash flow. Before Blatchford, he feels he was drowning in debt. With Blatchford, he established solid system to pay down debt and now pays himself regularly.

He works Monday, Tuesday and Wednesday. He is working 144 days. "I was contemplating moving the practice to the new location since it has a way better view than my current location. I was negotiating with the landlord of the merger practice for tenant improvement and lease term. I ended up deciding to stay put and the lease for the other space will expire shortly." On his fourth day, he does some administration and volunteer dentistry with Medical Teams International.

In his family, he is the cook. He and Liz make a point of involving their children in their errands and prep for cooking. They aim to have positive (PoFo) for Positive Conversations. Their weekends can be devoted to family. Piano lessons and Tai Kwan Do are the main kid activities. Liz is the musician. Because both dentists leave at 6:30 AM, they have a full time nanny who runs errands, picks up dry cleaning and takes kids to activities during the week but Ben looks forward to the cooking and eating together.

He feels his leadership is a work in progress. He admires the leadership of Drs. Josh Leute and Matt Fluegge. Ben feels they are firm in their statements. Ben finds there is still some drama with his team which occurs when the team does not reach bonus. Their highest bonus has been $1K and they average $500 to $700. When team misses it, that is when it is tough.

Dr. Wang feels Christina opened his eyes to possibilities. He has set a future vision. They both continue to improve themselves with readings, seminars with Tony Robbins. Before, he felt he was wandering aimlessly. He knows that hope is not a good growth strategy.

Ben shared one of the best benefits of Blatchford Coaching is an increase in net return. His family of five was able to go to Taiwan for ten days to visit his aging (we are all aging) mother and father. Ben was born in NY while his father earned a PhD in chemical engineering. The young family then returned to Taiwan where Ben and his brother went to school. At age 16, Ben felt he was doing poorly in the rigorous

Taiwanese education system so his Mom took the two boys to Fresno to complete high school and then to UC Davis and the rest is history.

His wife Liz had much the same progression. She was born in KS to Korean parents who went back to Korea when their education was completed. She returned to CA for high school. She and Ben met at Temple Dental School in Philadelphia. Interestingly, Ben's Fresno gang went to UCLA and became friends with Liz before she met Ben.

We love these stories and wish the Wangs the very best.

www.centerportdental.com

On our trip to Taiwan to visit Grandpa and Grandma.
PRICELESS!

Blatchford Game Plan: Cosmetics Anywhere?

Many dentists live for cosmetics and reconstruction—the cosmetic home run which will make a huge monetary difference in their monthly bottom line. How tightly niched can you be in cosmetics and still make a living? Can it work in every area, as touted by some?

Consider cosmetic work is not covered by insurance. Good because it then becomes your patient's choice. Because cosmetics are not insurance driven, a certain sophistication of skills and mastery in psychology in sales is necessary to have a general dentistry patient say "yes" to treatment not covered by their insurance. If your practice is insurance driven; mentally you and your staff are tied to insurance fees and maximums, it is a real challenge for optional cosmetics to have a great impact in your practice. If your staff knows each patient's insurance coverage by heart, it is an indicator insurance is the air in your office. It would be rare for a ten veneer case to happen in this practice, even if the doctor and team are highly clinically trained.

Because cosmetic and largely reconstructive work is non-insurance (in a $40,000 estimate, how much will be covered by their insurance?), mastering sales skills by each staff member, not just the doctor, will make or break your cosmetic acceptance. Unless sales are studied, mastered and applied with excellent open-ended questions asked with your patients dreaming into their future, the conversation will likely go the deep hole "technical route" of NEED and the patient will ask, "Why should I do this?" "Will my insurance cover this?" "Oh, no, I don't think so." "I am not interested." The cosmetically trained dentist thinks, "No one in my town is interested in cosmetics but I love learning."

Learning just the clinical techniques of cosmetics will not result in cases accepted. Study relationships, build trust, research psychology to discover why sales is a never ending process with every team member involved. Cosmetic success takes a paradigm shift for each team member.

Study the composition of your drawing area. Though we want to democratically make cosmetics available to everyone, there are some sets of people who are much more interested and can dream their dreams more easily with some "wiggle room" money. If your small area is the home to trust funders and wealthy transients, it may work for a tightly niched cosmetic and reconstructive dentist without general dentistry or even a hygiene program.

If, on the other hand, your smaller area is composed of solid blue collar citizens depending upon an annual harvest or the shaky continuation of the foundry for their living, your approach to cosmetics may come from their dream of saving their own teeth, not having teeth that come out at night and having teeth that work. To market strictly "cosmetics" may not work well. There is no "wiggle room" for these folks and they believe in longevity and value for their dollar. This practice will be successful with a solid general dentistry base and skills that offer value and longevity. An occasional home run will occur.

Dr. Brian Saby of Red Deer, Alberta, concurs. An accredited member of AACD, Brian had externally marketed, focusing on cosmetics. He discovered potential patients perceived cosmetics was all he did. Since the majority of his cosmetic work comes from regular patients who have been shown the possibilities, he changed the focus in his ads to attract the average patient.

What may work well is for the dentist to learn technical skills others may not be offering in the area, like automated endo, implant dentistry or cosmetic dentures.

Numbers and skill come into play. Cosmetic acceptance usually has a longer acceptance time. Thus there are huge oscillations in the income stream from month to month. Dr. Rhys Spoor of Seattle advises, "Cosmetics will naturally occur in a happy general practice. Pick the easy ones and feel great, referrals will come. Leave the hard ones for the dentists equipped to handle this and all the headaches which can result." Can you do cosmetics anywhere? Yes, but if that is exclusive, you may only work two days a month! Cosmetics anywhere? Yes and usually with a solid general dentistry base. Study your demographics before you niche your practice too tight. Make cosmetics a part of what you offer mixed with other services.

Bill Blatchford, DDS

From the Blatchford Play Book

Leaders work with the team to discover why there was success or if we failed, how can we create systems or conversations to not repeat that mistake. Dr. Wang feels he has a community practice. He is not anonymous in a big city and learning from successes and failures keeps a winning team moving forward.

Post Game

- Create phone skills, a tag line and message that set you apart. It is your first opportunity to impress. Be bold, be different

- Cross train each team member including the Doctor. Learn to answer the phone, make firm financial arrangements, have meaningful conversations about patient dreams, clean a room, run a day sheet, sharpen instruments, make appointments and operate the computer.

- Practice introducing guests to staff members, sharing what you have learned and making your guests feel special.

- Analyze plays which have not worked in your office. Make changes, build skills and reconstruct confidence to move forward

- When you have had a great game, replay it. What worked? Why did it work? How can we do it again?

- Analyze the time factor of how long a guest takes to build a relationship of trust, moving to acceptance

13

WINNING AS A SINGLE MOM

Dr. Laura Fauchier

Laura is mother to three girls, and a successful dentist in Marion, Iowa. Her time and efforts for her girls come first and she feels Blatchford Coaching has helped her create a practice which takes less time to produce more return.

Balance and time are critical to her mothering success. Laura is the main caregiver as well as the family breadwinner. She feels Blatchford has helped her be able to spend much more time with her three girls.

Laura grew up in Iowa with a family culture where women were meant to have children and stay home. Even before her babies were born, Laura went to work with Dr. Tracey Hughes in an all female practice as a part-time assistant. These were the first female dentists Laura had ever encountered. Tracey told her she had curiosity and talent and she should go to dental school.

Laura never had career aspirations and her family history was well established and being repeated. Laura has four sisters and two brothers where everyone is a parent and women stay home. She was taught that to fulfill her creation was to become a mother; to do something different would detract from her motherhood.

Laura, like so many, did not realize how poor the family situation was. She had grown up in a family with economic instability and this lack of funds continued into her own new marriage. By the time she realized she aspired to be a dentist herself, she already had two very young daughters. A third was born during dental school. Dr. Fauchier was married up through the year past her dental school graduation. During those school years, her husband was a student also and they lived on less than $1K a month. For childcare, she took out student loans and paid her sister to take care of her children. Fifty percent of her class was female. She thought she would be one of a few. She found all the women to be smart, lovely and kind. In the first week of her second dental year, she had a baby and the school told her she could take a week off or take the whole year off. The baby went to school with Laura. She has a picture of her oldest daughter in the simulator clinic with mannequins.

She graduated with $200K in student debt. The school awarded her a needs-based scholarship (she did not apply but the school must have noticed). Laura felt very guilty for bringing debt into her family. Her husband was very supportive of dental school and was a real hands-on dad. When Laura graduated, her husband was in the National Guard and was deployed twice overseas.

Laura became an associate and promised buyer for a practice in a small town eight months after graduation. The year was 2008 and not many practices were on the market. Immediately, she had disposable income and she had family close by.

Now, her practice usually produces between $130 and 170K monthly. "I used to have an associate; we now collect just a bit more than we did when we had him." Also, before, Laura worked 4 to 4.5 days per week and rarely took off more than a week or two plus a few days here and there. In 2016, they will have taken nine weeks. "We have added CAD/CAM, Kois training, laser including LANAP, sleep apnea, Invisalign, eliminated amalgam, increased our denture cases and fees, and most recently added minimal sedation."

It is her daughters whom she is most proud. Sally is the oldest and she feels dentistry is "gross" and wants to investigate neuropsychology at the University of Iowa. The middle daughter is Emma with a learning disability frequently associated with depression and anxiety. It is Non-Verbal Learning Disorder, similar to autism. She is in a special school in Idaho and Laura feels blessed that Blatchford Coaching has helped her have the extra funds to help her daughter. Emma is very talented at music and language, and is working on managing her worries at her private school. More time and more money is what Laura has to spend with her daughters. Mimi is the youngest. After training on treating sleep apnea, Laura had a hunch and decided to have her three daughters tested for sleep apnea and two now wear CPAPs and are so much more attentive and positive.

Laura is needed in her town. She has a nice location, good reputation and great Google reviews. She does not pay for SEO as in Iowa, she feels, is a very favorable place to practice. She does not need to market heavily. She takes Delta as well as Blue Cross/Blue Shield. She looks forward to being out of debt and letting the rest of the insurance contracts go.

Her team is all from the area, have excellent attitudes and high standards. The changes in team she made were hard. She realizes she is now strong in sharing her vision, her standards and the team has responded. She realized now that she was paying the price in time and effort without having strong leadership. With strong purpose, it has changed and her natural ability to lead has come forth. She thanks Blatchford every day for the transformation and can feel the ease of a practice well lead.

She realizes she did not have a clue what she would encounter in the next nine years—two deployments, a divorce, Emma and her special needs, and an abusive rebound relationship with an "opportunist." This became a legal problem with a permanent injunction resolution and Laura now feels she is in a better position to help other women. She realizes she can have a platform to help others recognize abuse. She is grateful to be in a position to give back, has an ear out for single moms and is in a position to help. She feels somehow, she is like a magnet and women do come to her. She is using the Blatchford Power Questions and in her conversations, she invites them to talk, and "tell me more."

Laura is now engaged to be married and is planning a wedding. She recently joined households with her fiancé and bonus daughter, Carleigh. She is grateful to be in a new family situation and enjoying once again having a partner to co-lead.

www.mariondental.org

Laura in her first dental job as a part time assistant. She was pregnant and wore the lead apron to protect her baby.

Laura with her three daughters at her dental school graduation.

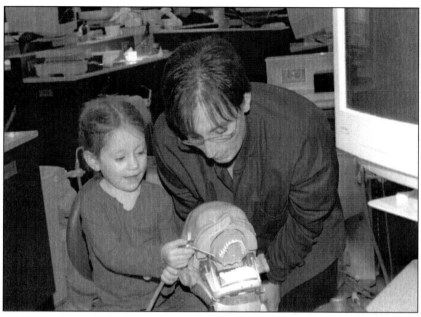

Laura and Sally in the Simulation room during her freshman year of dental school.

Laura and her "Littles"

Mike (Mr. Reliable) and Laura to be married fall 2017

Laura with her team

Blatchford Game Plan:
Reinventing Your Practice with Double the Results

When Dr. Fauchier purchased her practice in the area near her family, she had the opportunity to reinvent the practice. What does she want it to be in 20 years? Who does he want to be attracting? With Dr. Blatchford's help, she is moving from Point A to Point B and is doing very well, thank you.

What if your business burned down and you had the opportunity to reinvent it? Knowing what you know now, is there anything you're doing now that you wouldn't get into? Are there any relationships you would avoid?

Answers change but questions don't change. Therefore today, 70% of our past decisions have been wrong or below standard. There is a story of Albert Einstein, while teaching physics at Princeton, a student noticed the questions on the physics test were the same as last year. When confronted with this, Einstein said, "Yes, the questions are the same, but the answers are different."

We must be masters of change, demonstrating great flexibility. What it takes to successfully reinvent your business is intense future orientation. You must develop clarity for a five-year fantasy. With clarity, you increase the likelihood it will come true. Make a dream list. We must be strong in where we are going and flexible in the how. The future only matters, not the past. "You cannot jump across a canyon in two jumps." In other words, it is not possible to hang onto the past while looking to the future.

Any investment takes time, money and emotion. To achieve the fantasy, we must differentiate between facts and problems. Facts cannot change but problems can be solved. Focus on which are the most important solvable problems. How will you solve them to reinvent your practice?

Most major changes should have been made sooner. In other words, we have known of the problems in our practice for a while but failed to focus and make the appropriate decisions to create a different result. Andrew Grove, former President of Intel Corporation, said change *should* be done about a year before it is. To reinvent your practice in the next five years, decisions need to be made now.

Brian Tracy, author of *Eat that Frog*, had been selected to speak with over 100 graduates of Blatchford Coaching. We requested Mr. Tracy orient his remarks specifically to dentistry and presenting larger, optional treatment. Tracy created an electric presence, as his talk was so meaningful.

He said the three functions of an executive (you, the dentist) are to innovate and market, set and achieve goals, perform and get results. Results are everything. Set a goal to double your net income next year. You must be clear about the goal and flexible in the process.

To be the best, you must want to be the best. You must first have the desire to be the best. Average will no longer do. To achieve your goals of doubling your net income, ask yourself, the following:

- What business am I in? What business should I be in? What business could I be in?

- Who is my client? Today, tomorrow, who should be my client? Who could be my client?

- What does my client consider valuable? To feel better, to be happy?

- What do I do especially well? Today? Could? What should I be doing well?

- What are the constraints on doubling my income?

Tracy oriented his remarks to dentists who want to be in the top tier of dentistry. These dentists not only want to be the best, they want to be recognized as the best. The perception of quality is directly related to profitability. Everything counts and in creating the perception of quality, 20% is service and 80% is in the way that service is delivered. In other words, dentists can be excellent clinicians but the patient's perception of your clinical quality is based more on the delivery of that excellent service by you and your staff.

What is stopping you from doubling your net income next year? Obviously, increasing revenue and decreasing expenses is an answer but the focused use of our time makes a greater difference. Everyone believes his or her dance card is full. If we could change 10-20% of what we are doing, it can achieve an increase of 80-90% of profits. What should I discontinue doing? Stop doing things that others could do better.

Most dentists and staffs are on "task overload." We do things because "we've always done them this way." We fail to look outside the box to examine what is most important and how we could do it more efficiently.

Tracy said to fire "clients from hell" and focus on positive people. If a patient's visit doesn't go well, they tell 13 others. If it is good, they tell five people. Since everything counts and nothing is neutral, we must work to position our practice and ourselves in the marketplace. Think of a grid (series of squares) in the mind of your patient or potential patient. One of those boxes is you. What is in your box? What they see is what they think of you. What are they thinking and saying about you? What words would you choose to have them thinking or talking about you? How can we do more things to create this impression? Your customer's perception is the only thing that counts and it can be created either by design or by accident.

Everything counts and it takes continual mental preparation of each event. Keep asking yourself, what else? What else? When modest and humble Wayne Gretzky retired, he was asked to share the secret of his success. He said, "Maybe what separated me is that I had passion for the game," he said. "Secondly, I was dedicated to it. I prepared for every game and I always felt like I hadn't done enough. If I had three goals I wanted to get five goals. If I had seven points, I wanted to get eight. I approached each game as if it was a Stanley Cup game."

In sales, think of yourself as a consultant and partner to the patient. Ask good questions and listen. Make recommendations by including the patient, like "What WE should do next is"… "Our next step is...." Working as a partner and including the patient create urgency. Listening builds trust, which constitutes 40% of the sales process. Listen attentively, pause before replying, question for clarification ("how do you mean?") and give feedback by paraphrasing in your own words.

Bill Blatchford, DDS

From the Blatchford Play Book: Keep On Keeping On

With all good things going on in Laura's life, she is one to keep on. She is persistent and this is paying off for her financially and emotionally.

► You do not know which is the winning play of the day so play full out all the time

► As Winston Churchill said, "Never, never, never give up."

► Praise, monetary bonus, recognition make a huge difference in moving forward

► Any change in practice environment improves productivity according to the Hawthorne Study. Reupholster the furniture, paint the walls, new pictures all gain the team's attention.

► Keep reading a new book, CD, every week

► Don't quit until you've accomplished your goal

► Face each problem, solve it and move on.

► Each roadblock makes you a stronger person

► Keep knocking on the door of opportunity

► A man is never beaten until he thinks he is

► Life is a grindstone. What you're made of determines if it will grind you down or polish you up.

14

SMALL TOWN DENTIST

Dr. Angie Cotey

Dr. Cotey practices in a small town of 8K southeast of Madison, Wisconsin. Though she and her husband live in Madison, Mt. Horeb is important to her and her team and she makes a real effort to be involved in their town. Taking the Blatchford creed to heart to avoid being the "invisible dentist," she and her team make a real effort to be present all over town at festivals, community events, patronizing local businesses with their team jackets and logos, and being active members of the local Chamber of Commerce, Optimist Club and American Legion.

Angie is a graduate of Marquette Dental School with about 50% females in her class, and is the first dentist in her extended family. She has inspired several female cousins and nieces to be pre-dent majors. Her Marquette class was inspiring to create a culture of support and sharing which continues to exist today.

Angie always thought she would be a physical therapist in college, however after a mission trip to Jamaica working with dental students, she happily changed her focus to dentistry. When in dental school, she took the same Jamaican mission trip as a dental student.

Giving back has been important to Angie and she continues with mission trips and local charity events.

Angie was selected for the Navy scholarship at Marquette and served in Japan at a smaller base with five dentists, just an hour away from a much larger base. She and her husband were able to really travel while in Japan, an aspiration which continues for them. For Angie's birthday this year, she and two dental school classmates and travel buddies spent two weeks in Viet Nam.

After three years of military service, Angie and her husband wanted to return to Wisconsin and a smaller town. She originally thought she wanted to work for someone else so became an associate in a corporate practice. She was working five days a week and found she was unable to have Fridays off to take CE courses. She sought a classmate's counsel and Carson Kutsch told her, "Angie, you will only achieve your goals having your own practice. You can do this. Call Bill Blatchford and do everything he tells you."

She wanted to purchase a smaller practice and make it grow. By joining a local study club she networked and looked at many practices, however she was unsure the best way to evaluate a practice. Blatchford helped her find the perfect practice for her. It was producing $400K at purchase and in five years, she is at $800K.

Angie felt she had very little business preparation. She felt it was overwhelming for a new female business leader. What she likes about Blatchford and coaching is it keeps her on track and accountable to make progress each month and improve leadership skills. She feels Blatchford encouraged her to have strong big goals and to dream about what might be possible. The seminars inspire her and her team to reach for higher goals each time. Angie loves that she feels supported and not alone. She likes to bounce ideas off other Blatchford Doctors.

To make it work in her smaller town, she offers many procedures. She was the only female dentist until recently. She is only contracted with Delta Premier insurance which is the policy of the education system in Mt. Horeb. All three of her employees grew up in and are residents of the local area. In hiring, she looks for good ethics and self motivators who want to better themselves through goal setting and hard work, not those just looking for entitlements.

Her friends and family ask "when do you ever work? and why do you continue to take so many CE classes?" Angie is a Kois graduate, a big deal. She does implants and just purchased a cone beam. She does gum grafting, endo, ortho and Invisalign. Dr. Cotey does surgery and extractions. She is just completing a two year program at USDI and has started to offer regular ortho to children in her practice. Word moves fast in her small town and she does not really need to market. To gather orthodontic patients, the word is already out there and they are getting many internal referrals.

She has made a real point of showing local art in her practice. She and her team have a strong esprit de corps by celebrating any and all occasions in their practice, dressing up and having a fun environment. They enjoy their connections with patients and their community.

She feels Blatchford sets some pretty high standards for achievement. Her next big goal is to work on systems to have them smooth and maximize their time in the office to continue to grow and take even more time off as well as a team vacation. On her two-week Viet Nam experience, she booked her trip six months out. Other adventures have been to South Africa, Italy, sailing the British Virgin Islands, Hawaii, Alaska, Thailand, and annual ski trips out west. She is enjoying a work life balance that was made possible through the Blatchford systems.

www.villagesmilecare.com

Photographing Victoria Falls in Zimbabwe

Angie in her military uniform

At Sankei-en Garden in Japan with husband Dave

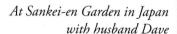

Family photo, boating on Lake Monona, our favorite pastime

Dressed up as tooth fairies for an event

Blatchford Game Plan: Your Agenda Costs You

Dr. Cotey and team practice in a small town and have worked extensively on their sales skills. They know they cannot talk a patient into treatment. They know if they begin the conversation with their idea of how this person should look, it will ruin the sale. They work very hard to allow the patient's ideas and dreams to be what drives the conversation. Not only is this more successful, the patient feels heard and included.

A dentist is so technically trained that it inhibits the sales process. A dentist is constantly designing in their mind what their idea of a perfect smile would be for a new patient, the grocery clerk, the spinning instructor, and the waiter. You can't help it! And, this is what makes the end result so excellent. However, you trip over your own feet in the sales process when you already have a picture in mind for your patient. Your agenda will cause you to stumble.

The sales process (the time before a patient says "yes") has no opening for your agenda or picture of what you think a person should look like. How can you have any listening when you already have your mind made up? For a successful sale on any item, the value must be present. If the buyer has little idea of what is possible, our job is to ask questions and uncover those hidden values. Our job is to help the buyer deepen their values and give them what they want. If you already have in mind what you want them to want, a successful sale will likely not take place.

In the sales world, they refer to dentists as "non-selling health care professionals." Our technical training creates a natural path of educating our patient into submission. We draw pictures on bracket covers and speak with words not understood on the street. Another paradigm we hold is our patients NEED to have this treatment. Non-selling health professionals thus talk our patients into understanding the treatment we think they need.

The end result is, the patient accepts only what they think they NEED right now. They are not exposed to dreaming about their idea of a beautiful smile or chewing with comfort. The result is a little treatment is accomplished on many people. The dentist and staff continue to run from chair to chair. The dental zoo endures.

Dentists are not the only carriers of agenda overload. Staffs also subscribe. How can you tell? When you see the picture of Vince Lombardi, what are your immediate thoughts? The Boat Salesman of the Year said he attributes his success to "I never begin with a boat in mind." Do you begin with a smile in mind?

For a successful sale, the technically trained must clear their minds of their own agendas. Our job is to help the patient uncover their agenda. Develop a trusting relationship by staying out of the "tooth talk" while you develop a friend. Ask questions to uncover their hobbies, if they are new in town, what interests them. Dr. Bob Barkley said, "You can never sell anything to a stranger."

By asking questions, you help your patients uncover their own agenda. You must think of your mind like a blank canvas and the patient is painting a picture for you. This is where we have our wires crossed. We think we need to paint the picture for the patient. This is our pitfall in sales as the "non-selling health care professional."

Ask your patient a future focus question rather than the usual, "do you have any concerns today?" Ask what they would like their smile or dental health to be like in twenty years? Now, you are making them think with the right side of their brain, the dream side, and the decision side. Their predictable answer is the desire to keep their own teeth. Ask why. Probe deeper. Ask more questions. Keep asking questions like, "What benefits could you see by keeping your own teeth?" "Tell me about your dental heritage." "Is keeping your teeth a family tradition?"

If you keep asking questions, the patient will paint a picture for you. They will tell you what is important to them. Their answers will sound like looking good, younger, better or lasting a long time and/or feeling good. Ask them to expand on those thoughts. Show your after pictures to help them visualize their dream smile. Have them describe it and share what advantages they could see by having a smile like that.

If you allow the patient to paint their picture, they will own it. If you arrive with your agenda in mind for them, they will not see it for themselves. You will end up putting unwanted pressure on your patient to accept what you had in mind. Create the opportunity for your new friend to dream out into the future about their smile. Have them describe it and they will own it. For greater success, drop your agenda for them.

Bill Blatchford, DDS

From the Blatchford Play Book: Jump and Shout

External marketing is branding yourself as different, which has been the very antithesis of established dental circles. You may be the first. It takes courage, boldness and a real sense of self. Dr. Angie Cotey utilizes ingenuity in becoming known.

- ► Be a participant in your community, not an observer
- ► Have a great website and host
- ► Be enthusiastic about life
- ► Think of marketing as helping your community be stronger
- ► Everyday think of small ways to improve your practice
- ► Get excited about dentistry. Be thrilled you chose to improve people's lives
- ► Use the radio for getting the word out
- ► Take part in festivals, fairs, art shows, etc
- ► Place media ads in well-read publications
- ► Get professional help with the design
- ► Have a visible location with excellent signage
- ► How about "community service" digital clock, temperature sign at your office?
- ► Wave the flag
- ► Sponsor a ball team
- ► Become the local dental expert by giving talks on dentistry
- ► Join a service club and be active
- ► Look for ways to do business locally

15

THE TEACHER

Dr. Kim Okamura

Dr. Okamura is the energizer bunny. She is five feet tall and all of 98 pounds with her favorite sport being basketball. We feel, pound for pound, Dr. Okamura is a most profitable dentist with an overhead of 57%.

Practicing in the north Seattle area, Kim has purchased and combined three practices in her 28 years of practice. Since the 'A' Game's first publication, Kim has reached her earlier set goals of profitability and life balance. Her new goals are: to increase her production, collection and net by 5% each year, and enjoy more time with family.

Clearly, one of Kim's outstanding qualities is her clarity of vision and her ability to communicate her vision with passion and enthusiasm. She sees the bigger picture, knows where she is going, has a specific number of goals and, consequently, a great team that is attracted to the challenge. Dr. Okamura tends to have long-term staff that share her pace, vision, and demand excellence of themselves. She is the coach.

As a female professional, we feel she has worked through the leadership challenges. Her team knows this is a business. Dr. Okamura hires staff for strengths and she believes in their abilities. She lets her staff know it is OK to make mistakes. In fact, she encourages them to step out and be uncomfortable. When a task or conversation is not up to par, she communicates with the question, "What did you learn from this? If a similar situation arose, what would you do differently?" She expects and receives 200%. She is fiercely loyal to her team and really believes in them.

That said Dr. Okamura feels she is so loyal, she hangs on too long. One of her pitfalls as a leader has been becoming emotionally attached to people vs. a business-like attachment to the practice. As a leader, she feels she could make those tough staff decisions earlier. She has a time-table for new staff to learn skills, read books, be accountable and apply themselves for results. Kim pushes herself and expects the same from team. They read sales and marketing books, practice sales conversations, tape themselves and improve. It is all about practice, practice, practice. In practicing the sales skills, she likes to play the "what if" game, creating scenarios of possibilities. What if a guest said…, how would you respond? Her staff always participates in the monthly Blatchford staff conference call, sharing and learning from others. Kim uses "fireside chats" and believes that learning and implementation is a big part of being a team member.

Kim has reached her goal to practice three days a week so she can balance her life with family and fun. This had been a real challenge for Kim as she loves being a good mother, great wife and taking time for herself. She works at the balance. Her husband, Tim had owned and operated three 7/11 stores and now is into commercial real estate investments. The Okamura family lives in Redmond, WA (home of Microsoft) so Kim commutes 30 minutes across Lake Washington to work. She feels this distance has not affected her cosmetic attraction as her practice has 19K cars a day pass her office and her marketing is aimed at Greater Seattle market. Currently, she has huge poster-size copies of her current ads in her windows. Kim practices three days a week. The fourth day is designated as an administrative day. Time is blocked to complete treatment plans, communicate with clients and other health practitioners. It also serves as a day to write handwritten notes to clients and other marketing endeavors.

Kim's foray into dentistry was circuitous. Dr. Okamura is the oldest of five children of first generation American-born Chinese immigrants to Seattle. As the oldest, much was expected of her with the emphasis on education. While being fiercely independent and unfocused in grade school, she eventually buckled down and won an academic/track scholarship to Seattle Pacific. Her father was very disappointed when she chose not to continue after her first semester. Instead, she took a year long dental assisting course and while working for a year, she was encouraged to take her hygiene prerequisites and was accepted. At the same time, her professors encouraged her to apply to dental school and she was one of seven women graduates in the class of 1987 at the University of Washington. Her motivating factor was encouragement from others. Is there a lesson here?

Tim patiently waited for the focused Dr. Okamura to complete dental school before marriage. Kim felt she wanted to practice three years before having children but they came earlier. She took three months off, hired a locum, and grandparents insisted "no daycare" so they cared for their grandson while Kim continued to build her practice. A daughter was born several years later with the loving pattern established. Son and daughter are now young adults, both having graduated from college and are happily moving forward with their next life adventures!

All three practice purchases were within a one mile radius. Initially, she purchased a small family practice on the decline from a retiring dentist for $85K. She worked hard to build it up and after two years was looking for "what else?" A dentist with a good reputation was retiring for health reasons and with $135K practice purchase, she moved into his larger and more modern facility with one staff. After seven years in practice, she paid full fee of $225K for a practice with plans to renovate and move to this more visible and convenient location. This turned out to be the most uncomfortable purchase as the selling doctor (unknown to Kim) had not told his staff, his receptionist wife or hygienist daughter about selling. When Kim arrived to meet them, it was announced and there was immediate distrust and upset. Dr. Okamura feels she lost about 20% of the patients as she re-formed her team and found a facility to attract cosmetic possibilities and had it remodeled.

She is five minutes from I-5, the major North/South corridor, close to busy Northgate Mall with Nordstrom as the anchor store and close to the University district. It is a stand alone one-story leased building with parking and so very visible. Kim feels practice purchases are a sure way to add opportunities to a practice. Even today, she is mindful of the possibilities.

Dr. Okamura coaches to meet goals as she is basically supporting the family with Tim in commercial real estate investments. This is a numbers game. They want to gross $1M, netting half. They want to do a full mouth case once a quarter. This means attracting and diagnosing about four a quarter to meet that goal. Her external marketing, website and networking bring in the larger cases. Internal marketing, service, conversations and comfort keep existing guests referring their friends and family to Dr. Okamura. Her current crown fee is $1574 and veneer fee ranges from $1870 to $2200. Hygiene goal is $2000 a day, three days a week.

Updating and upgrading is constant. Kim has studied with Doctors David Baird, Ron Zokol, Louis Malcmacher and John Kois. She has completed studies at The Las Vegas Institute, the Pacific Implant Institute, Oral Sedation with DOCS, facial esthetics with the American Academy of Facial Esthetics and the Kois Center for Advancing Dentistry Through Science. Her mentors include Dr. Bill Blatchford and her father and several seasoned dental professionals. Her computer software is SoftDent. Her five-year goals are greater practice growth through listening and verbal skills, achieving more closing which means more bonusing for staff and even further evolving her practice in cosmetics, facial esthetics, implants, sedation, Invisalign and general dentistry.

Since moving to her new space in 1999, Kim has focused on marketing excellence. Her marketing budget is 6% of gross. She has created memorable right-brained print ads in Seattle magazines, bus backs and her website of www.kimokamuradds.com. Catch the energy in Kim's photo. Kim also has an e-newsletter which is so appropriate for computer-based Seattle. Dr. Okamura has three patients a week enter her practice through her website and internal marketing. Notice the consistency in marketing and presentation of her logo, name of practice is same as website and same on letterhead and throughout. The message is straightforward and not confusing.

Dr. Okamura coaches to the numbers, and profitability is the result. She feels being profitable is a distinct goal and anyone can do it if they set their mind to it. Her practice is a distinction because of her different life experiences—each has pushed her to new levels each time. Dr. Okamura's cosmetic and general practice has come by vision and careful design. She strongly believes in order to grow and thrive, you need:

- An advocate like Bill Blatchford to coach you to success

- Clinically excellent and extensive skills to "walk your talk"

- Confidence, be a risk taker, be creative, like new challenges, understand the culture and psychology of your clients' needs and desires and REALLY WANT IT!

- Communication skills to build team and to converse with your guests

- Strong and focused marketing

"You must watch your numbers and carefully plan. Do not buy the big toy when you have a good month. Be prepared for the big case by thinking and behaving with readiness." She leads by encouraging her team to "focus on the big picture and the little things will take of themselves.

Dr. Okamura finds it fascinating to observe subtle changes in her practice. Currently, she is seeing more guests arrive who have done their research homework on the internet and with friends. They arrive knowing what they want and they have selected Dr. Okamura to do the work.

www.kimokamuradds.com

Jumping to new heights is Dr. Kim Okamura. This picture is from her website and patients have said, "I chose you because you look like fun."

To be on top of her game, marketing has been key. View an Okamura ad at the back of the book.

Blatchford Game Plan: Ten-Year Plan

Dr. Okamura is a goal setter. Purchasing three practices and molding them into one highly niched cosmetic practice didn't just happen. Kim and her team know five years out of their marketing budget, their continuing education courses and equipment purchases as it is all on a schedule. A ten-year plan is an excellent map for any aspiring dentist.

Ten years from now, at the beginning of 2027, how well will you have guided and pushed your practice and life towards the goals and principles you have set? Or will 2027 bring another year repeating the same mistakes and small thinking of many other years? The choice is yours: to plan with diligence, develop new skills, commit with a vengeance and create outstanding results or to bump along and hope things will change for the better.

Every astute businessperson will share with you the positive energy and great results that occur when you take the time to develop a Ten Year Plan. It is really a map of where you want to go. Start by writing down how old you will be in 2027, the age of your spouse and each child. Just that act alone will shock you into action.

Why Ten Years? By projecting ten years out, the problems and objections of today disappear. What are our objections? Time and money are the two main "reasons" why we don't tackle our main obstacles today. By creating an ideal practice and great life ten years into the future, we eliminate the big barriers of today and can focus on smaller steps we need to take to achieve our ten year goals. Big goals seem more possible when you project ten years out.

The Ten-Year Plan stems from a real knowledge about yourself, your philosophy and where you are going in life. We call this your personal vision and it spills over directly into your practice life, also. What are your values? What is passionately important to you? What difference are you trying to make for yourself, your family, your patients?

What are the five most important values in your life? What do you stand for? What are the organizing principles of your life? What are your core beliefs? What virtues do you aspire to? What will you not stand for? What would you sacrifice for, suffer for and even die for?

Put them in order of priority. When you observe your own behavior and actions, they indicate to you what are your real values. These values will shape your life and practice in achieving your Ten-Year Plan.

The Ten-Year Plan should start with your personal life as your practice is a portion of your life, not the whole. Work is a most important focus and there must be a balance so you have a wonderful family and personal life, too.

It is important you write and speak this Ten-Year Plan as if January 2027 is now. If you are now 47 years old, you would say, "I am 57 years old" rather than "I hope" or "I will." Speak as if you already have accomplished your Ten-Year Plan.

In addition to your age, set a goal for your physical life. What is your weight in 2027? What is your heart rate, your cholesterol count, your resting pulse? What have you accomplished physically by 2027? Are there some new skills or new levels of accomplishment which you have achieved physically? Martial arts, climbing, hiking, running, biking?

List your children and what they have accomplished in 2027. Occupations, college graduations, your grandchildren? What hobbies do you have or are developing? Where have you traveled? What strong friendships have you developed? Describe your life in 2027. Are you married? Where are you living? Describe your home, location and features. Describe your spiritual life and involvement.

Concentrate now on your practice. Where is your practice located in 2027? What does the office look like? What high tech equipment do you have? What is the niche in the market you are appealing to? What is your reputation in the community? Who do you work with and what have they accomplished? How long has your staff worked with you? To whom do you refer?

What are your technical accomplishments in 2027? Are you an accredited member of a prestigious and rigorous course or organization? Are you a graduate of courses in areas of dentistry for which you have become known? How have you become a leading member of the dental community?

Specifically in your practice, who are your patients? What is your average case size? What attracts patients to you? How many days a year do you practice? What is your percentage of overhead? What does your practice day look and feel like? Are you focused on fewer patients and accomplishing more? What are your accounts receivables? What is your acceptance rate for your suggested treatment? What skills have you learned in the last ten years to be able to accomplish this?

What plans did you make in 2017 for your retirement funding? What will that total and how did you invest that money? By 2027, are you financially free of debt? What are your plans for retirement?

If you are not still practicing in 2027, what is your exit strategy? Did you develop a solid plan for a good transition for your patient care? If you are practicing in 2027, what is your transition plan for your practice? Will you leave your practice completely or will you still have a selective practice seven to ten days a month? What is the arrangement?

A Ten-Year Plan needs to be specific and real. When you take the time to write as if it is 2027 and dream about what might be possible, without the constraints and barriers of 2017, your dream can become a reality. The specifics in the Ten-Year Plan become the basis for concrete goals. These are then broken down into ten-year, five-year and one-year goals and then, even projects. If you want to have specific things happen in your practice and your life by 2027, what skills and preparation do you need to start now to have mastered that area by 2027?

Be outrageous. Dentists are held back by some constraints that are unnecessary and unwanted. If you could have your life and practice anyway you wanted, how would it be? Plan now for 2027 and you won't be disappointed.

Bill Blatchford, DDS

From the Blatchford Play Book: Winning Team

Dr. Okamura is a real teacher. Her mission in life is to help others see the possibilities in themselves. For that, she is a winner and her team is the recipient of patience, prodding and practicing. She is part of the winning team.

► Be accountable for mistakes and learn from them. This makes you more valuable to the team

► Hire people smarter than you

► Spontaneously sing praises of each other and doctor

► Be generous with compliments to each other

► Every patient has firm financial arrangements before receiving an appointment

► Think about your actions, conversations, body language and how that reflects your leader's vision

► Winning is a choice and there are many winners

► Action may not always bring happiness; but there is no happiness without action

► Practice, practice, practice

► It's the fundamentals

► You get out in front and you stay out in front

16

CHARACTER COUNTS

Dr. Christopher Maestro

Being physically fit from training for and running marathons as well as being financially fit and confident due to the preparedness imparted by his association with Blatchford Solutions, Chris Maestro was able to rest and heal without worry from the injuries sustained in a terrible automobile accident in the Autumn of 2015. While Chris was out of the practice for six weeks and working part time at best for another six weeks, the team of Maestro Dentistry performed miracles running the practice and properly taking care of patients during his recovery. Had it not been for the philosophies and standards established by being a part of Blatchford Solutions, the team and the practice would have been in an untenable position and perhaps near failure.

When Dr. Maestro first came to the Blatchford Summit, his wife Dianne asked of him, "what are you going to do differently this time to make this work?" Chris had been through two previous practice management programs yet with limited results. "This time it's going to be different because the Blatchford Program is not about which system to use to schedule and how to sell more dentistry, it's more about the doctor and team's personal and professional growth. I will get out of it

exactly what I put into it…if it's to be better, I've got to make it better."
Chris admitted that he really didn't know what he was made of and what
he was capable of before he began his coaching with Bill Blatchford.

Chris realized that all the successes of dental school and all the
clinical expertise attained did not necessarily translate into business
success. With the Blatchford's help, Chris was able to dig down deep
and make some big positive changes. It wasn't easy. Bill challenged him
early in the program by asking "just why is it that you aren't getting
the job done?" "Bill knew I had the potential but was getting my own
way. I had to make some very difficult decisions, I had to dream big,
I had to be confident of my own success. I didn't feel that I could ever
accomplish what Bill was recommending, ever."

One of those recommendations was to become a better dentist.
Bill recommended attending the Kois Center for Advanced Dentistry
in Seattle. Travel costs, tuition, time away from the practice…could
he ever afford this and did he deserve it? Today, Chris had completed
the course work with John Kois, has graduated from the program and
is planning to become a Kois Mentor in 2017. "This kind of personal
and professional growth is empowering" Chris is very happy to say.

"I truly feel that the Blatchford Coaching is not about money. It's
about living the life you want to and getting your practice to function
so that it can support you while you do. It's about lifestyle." Having the
correct team members is essential to reach the goals of the doctor and
the practice. Assembling the correct team, taking exceptional care of the
practice's patients and steering the practice to success and maintaining
that success is about leadership. "Bill has taught me how to be a visionary
and a leader; how there's no bad teams, just bad leaders. I am a much
better person, leader, and dentist having met and worked with Bill."

One measure of success was Chris' ability to retire $435K of practice
and personal debt over the less than five years he had been a part of the
Blatchford Program. "Being debt free was not something I thought I
would be so soon and in five years I was able to do so by providing better dental care for my patients and leading my team to reach their goals

and the practice goals." After a brief drop in bonus during his recovery, the team quickly attained bonuses up to $1,500.00 per team member.

His recent accident and the resultant time away from his office could have been a lot more damaging to his practice without the incredible team of four at Maestro Dentistry. Nancy, Cherie, Kara, and Erin now help to steer the successes in the practice. They are a real team working together and striving to improve all the time. The previous team of seven could never have managed what this "dream team" can. Even after missing the last six weeks of 2015, the practice still enjoyed a twenty percent increase in production and collections over 2014 and with almost ten weeks off. The team is self motivating and teach each other. They actively embrace the use of the Blatchford Power Questions and the Risk Assessment criteria of the Kois Center. The Blatchford concept of "Fries with that Burger" is a part of the daily repertoire. Chris is impressed with their confidence and finds they insist on an effective morning huddle and rewarding evening meeting.

With the help and assistance of the Blatchford Coaching Program, Maestro Dentistry is a fee for service practice. The practice has developed a reputation for exceptional service. The team has worked to reduce A/R to <$7K> from an A/R of $60K. They are producing approximately $108K per cycle with four team members. And, this year they will be taking 10 weeks off including a week at Thanksgiving and two weeks at Christmas. Congratulations Team Maestro!

Chris and his wife Dianne, along with another couple were on their way to the airport in Seattle after attending a Kois Center course. While the other passengers escaped serious harm, Chris unfortunately suffered a broken collarbone, eight fractured ribs (four broken in two places), a lacerated liver, a perforated lung, and a torn ligament in his left knee. Ouch! The only way home back to New York…a 66-hour train ride over hill and dale.

One very important benefit of a well run practice…more family time. Chris is thrilled to be able to take his family on vacations never thought possible and now has the time and ability to spend more time with his son Ryan (a NY State Trooper) and Ryan's wife Lisa (parents of Landon aged 5 and Grant aged 2.5), his son Kieran (PhD candidate in Psychology), and his daughter Cailee (graphic artist). The family Yorkshire Terrier even gets more attention now too.

His confidence in the Blatchford Coaching Program's ability to help dentists reach their goals led Chris to refer his Kois classmate, Dr. Brenon Farmer, to the program. Chris feels fortunate and blessed to have mentors such as Bill Blatchford and John Kois. "Because of the influence and mentorship of both Bill and John my dentistry, my practice, and my life are all so much better. Thank you to you both!"

www.maestrodentistry.com

The Maestro Team: Nancy, Kara, Dr. Maestro, Cherie, Erin

Dr. Maestro with his mentor, Dr. John Kois, receiving his completion certificate

Blatchford Game Plan: A Winning Staff

Dr. Maestro has been blessed with winning staff and longevity, a successful combination.

Relationships with patients are stronger, emotional ties to each other are invaluable and the team feels they have a higher calling.

Contrast this with the "revolving door" which occurs in some practices. Case acceptance is more of a struggle, team bonding is challenged and the bigger picture gets lost. What are the factors which allow the team to dedicate their professional lives to this practice? Is it luck or a factor of his leadership skills and a life filled with grace?

We dream of THE team! How do you gather people who will hold your vision as precious and treat patients special? From 8 to 5, we need a team with no "I" in it. We need enthusiasm, sophistication, warmth, brains and an internally motivated work ethic.

An average dentist can continue with an average staff where conversations and logistics are gathered from previous average dentists and the cycle continues. As dentistry has changed from crisis care to optional choices, the staff composition must change, also.

Upon driving into their lot, Les Schwab, the largest independent tire dealer in America, has staff run to your car to help. The building and store is immaculate and the staff all wears clean white shirts. How does he find such great workers? Les Schwab says "you cannot train people to have a good attitude. You have to select them."

If you want your staff to shine, you must select people who have the internal qualities you desire. You can train them in the technical dentistry. Of course, there are no guarantees in life, however, ask the questions and observe the structure of responses.

I would want self-confidence as a quality. Can they look you in the eye with warmth and shake your hand? Do they stand tall and dress with proper decorum? Is there enthusiasm and optimism present? Are they givers or takers? If they ask you a benefit question before they share what they are willing to do for you, this may be a clue.

Dentistry is now a people game. Are they comfortable being in a conversation with you? Do you use proper grammar and speak clearly in complete sentences? Would this person be able to relate to all ages? There is not a position available in good dental offices where you have no patient contact or important conversations. Everyone must be comfortable with different people.

Curiosity is an excellent trait. Do they ask questions? Business guru Tom Peters says "Hire curious people." Staffs that are willing to step outside the box are usually willing to go beyond routine and be accountable for the results.

Discover their ability to be multi-dimensional by asking what book they are currently reading or what is their latest hobby? People are more interesting to others (your guests) when there is something going on in their life. Would you take this person on a trip across West Texas in a non air-conditioned VW bus?

Find out their picture of accountability by asking what they are responsible for now? How do they feel about owning their results? What is being "responsible" on a team?

Of course, cleanliness and order are very important. Personal grooming can be a reflection. Purses, cars and wallets are other indications of order and cleanliness. Check in the parking lot and have them use a pen from their purse during the interview.

Because dentistry is changing, determine their flexibility by asking some hypothetical questions like learning a new computer program or remodeling to work in a different area. Find people with a sense of adventure. Someone who cannot change will be like an anchor in your office.

Because dentistry is a business, your staff needs to be comfortable dealing with money and fees. Find out their own deserve level by asking questions. Is it ok with them for a guest to choose to spend $20,000 to improve their smile? Would you consider it for yourself? A personal deserve level is an invisible floor and ceiling which we feel we could not penetrate in material goods, relationships, fun, or our lives. We need teams who believe in your product.

You would follow the interview with a working interview. Have them work in your office for a day or two. If the basic characteristics that are important to you are present, you may find an excellent team mate. If after 10 days you discover they really interview well and there are some basics that concern you, consider finding a new staff member. Brian Tracy in *Maximum Achievement* said, "We know at least a year before we actually let someone go. This is costly in terms of your leadership as your team already knows who is playing the game well."

Finding the right team is a continual game. Keeping them is another story.

Bill Blatchford, DDS

From the Blatchford Play Book: Character Counts

We have heard others say, "Dr. Maestro is a fine person." In building a practice and team, his basic character shows and it does count.

- ▶ Look for honesty, respect and unselfishness
- ▶ Look for people who stand for something
- ▶ Surround yourself with positive people, get rid of negativity
- ▶ Don't live in the "gray areas." An issue is either black or white, right or wrong
- ▶ Never compromise what you think is right
- ▶ To live a perfect day, you must do something for someone who will never be able to repay you
- ▶ Keep your promises
- ▶ Take care of your reputation
- ▶ You are in charge of your attitude
- ▶ Be real; walk your talk
- ▶ Be the best you can be
- ▶ Never compromise your integrity
- ▶ Remember, no one makes it alone—have a grateful heart and be quick to acknowledge those who help you
- ▶ Step up to the plate and be accountable for your actions. Take responsibility for the good things you do as well as the mistakes and failures
- ▶ Become the most positive and enthusiastic person you know
- ▶ Never cheat, lie or steal
- ▶ Look people in the eye

17

THE HIGHLY NICHED PRACTICE

Dr. Rhys Spoor

What makes Dr. Spoor different is his passion, his intensity, his desire to keep learning and sharing plus his commitment to excellence. Rhys and his team will produce $1.6M in three 8-hour days a week, has a credit balance at all times working with five full time staff. His is a highly niched aesthetic, implant, restorative and TMD practice on the 46th floor of a Seattle high-rise filled with lawyers and financial institutions. The draw from the building has always been relatively small because he does not participate in any of the dental insurance plans, thus making the 4000 plus daily occupants of the building not look to his practice as a place for regular dental care. Consequently, his marketing budget is nearly 8%; his patients arrive looking for a smile change.

They average 10-15 new consults a month, depending on the success of external marketing. He has three days a week of hygiene as his guests come into the practice for aesthetics or are referred for a specific reason. The goal of hygiene has evolved into a broader control of chronic inflammation to improve the oral and systemic health of every patient.

Some doctors desire to have a cosmetic practice like Rhys' and easy is what it might appear. A cosmetic practice without a general dentistry base can have great fluctuations in time and money based on patient entry, acceptance, delivery and completion. In 2008, when the economy took a big downturn, so did the discretionary spending of many of his potential patients and there were a few years that were lean. But going back to the principles of putting the patients best interest first and delivering the highest quality care that he and his team knew how to do, the practice bounced back. Rhys has by choice basically eliminated general dentistry for smile design and complex restorative cases.

Seattle has many fine clinicians in a drawing population of a million plus. Branding, advertising and marketing are at a high level in Seattle and each year becomes increasingly more sophisticated.

He does not compromise in his treatment. He treats people exactly as he and his team would like to be treated. "I don't offer anything I wouldn't offer to my wife, Margaret, our children or my parents. My standards don't change based on the fact they pay for what I suggest. Ultimately, it is up to the patient to decide 'yes' or 'no' and I always try to give them a range of options that meet their desires and explain the risks and benefits of each option, including doing nothing. When you empower the patient to make their own informed choice they often choose what I present as the best option. I practice at the best level I know to do for everyone and I'm continually learning. The dentistry I do next year will compare differently from what I am able to do today. As technology changes, techniques are better and I get better. I want to keep incorporating all these changes for every patient, just as I do for my family."

Dr. Spoor's style of leadership reflects his intensity, excellence and passion. "I have been known by a number of people who work with me to be extremely demanding. I make no excuses or apologies. I am demanding on myself and I'm demanding of the people who work with me. However, I am fair and very clear on what is expected and what is accepted. I expect their best efforts constantly. I expect each of them to strive for excellence as I do myself. I expect them to be honest, trustworthy and punctual. I'm direct and tend not to sugar-coat things. For some people, this is great. For others, this doesn't work at all."

"I have worked hard to assemble a team that truly sees their professional world as I do. We all have similar goals, standards and great communication. We work pointedly to keep improving how we can be more effective in communicating between ourselves and with our patients by having monthly meetings just on that subject. I do well with people who are proactive, take responsibility for themselves and are willing to take appropriate and necessary risks."

"There have been times in my career when I worked with staff that had much different goals than mine. My hardest decision was firing a staff member for the first time. She was my receptionist, had worked with me for ten years and I liked her. I realized she just didn't have the ability to create the relationship with patients that we wanted to be there for the type of practice we were building. We had training sessions, workshops and scripting but she just didn't have the characteristics to make it work. I really liked her and wanted her to make it. I finally had to tell her we couldn't work together any more. It was the hardest thing I ever did."

"My definition of success has changed over time. When I first started, success meant making money. Therefore, very successful meant making a lot of money. But the financial aspect is just a part of the overall success equation. There are other components that are even more important and they include family and friends, health, spirituality, education, travel, knowledge, wisdom and generosity. Success is based on how happy you truly are. Since we're at this job so many waking hours and days of our lives, being happy at work is a real definition of being successful to me. When I am happy at my work, we make more money which can buy us more time off. As much as I love what I do, I love the time off. Margaret and I love to travel, experience new cultures, do lots of things; that is where success really comes through. A number of individuals in our lives have passed away and we are getting older that happens more often. Never did I hear, 'I wish I would have spent more time at the office.' The time we do spend at work needs to be happy so you do not regret that time. You cannot buy that time back no matter how much money you make. My father, who is now 83 and worked harder than anyone I have ever known for 50 years before he retired told me recently to enjoy every day because they only come once."

The five full-time team members all have learned to work together and cover for each other when needed. It is a synergy that has been purposefully created and constantly re-examined and altered as necessary.

"When we are on, we're on and everyone can feel it. In our 'A' game, things just flow. It feels good to be there because you know you're prepared and patients are receiving optimal care. Everyone is having a good time and the guests can feel it. There is a definite plan and it is like watching ice dancers. It is all choreographed. You have to know your part of the routine; it is not random. You also have the clinical ability to allow yourself to take divergent paths to reach the end point. Obstacles are challenges to go around but they do not halt the process. Every case has these challenges in some form or another. Even when the flow is going, you have to expect obstacles. Part of playing your 'A' game is having a plan of what you'll do when it becomes your 'B,' 'C' or even 'D' game."

Rhys feels he is profitable because he now sets long range and short term goals. He feels that is a natural progression of being older and seeing a finite time for your own life. He feels strongly anyone can be successful and profitable no matter your practice location. "You must define who you are, decide what is important to you and set your own goals. As much as I enjoy my career, it's not the primary thing I do in my life. It's an avenue I use to get the things I enjoy—time, travel, and choices. Yet, I want to be happy at work and that is where we are now. We really enjoy the days at work and we are happy to be away from it." It is a balancing act of serving your client base and buying time away."

Many dentists want to duplicate Rhys' staff. Collecting a team of excellence requires a leader who is focused; willing and skilled in communicating expectations with clarity and praise. One young dentist recently told Blatchford, "I want my staff to praise me like Rhys' team members do. I want them to sell me." Rhys would tell you, "the team road is a long adventure. I have been blessed and I have done my share of replacing. I have been guilty of holding on, hoping it would work out. I have created a high level practice of choice. Therefore, I must have a team who is able the play the game full out for as Brian Tracy says, 'Everything counts.'"

What motivates his staff? Certainly money as this is a job. "The people I work with are well paid but stay because of many other factors like respect, satisfaction and a sense of making a positive difference. Three of my team have now returned to work with me again after leaving the practice for anywhere from 1-8 years because of moving from the area. They came back willingly and with a different perspective from their experiences while they were gone. My current team enjoys a condensed work week and 10-12 weeks of time off with pay. They truly enjoy their jobs even though it is hard work."

Bottom line, Rhys warns the pitfalls of all this is if you can't communicate well; lack direction with leadership skills and keep the wrong staff around for your unspoken goals, your job as a dentist can be miserable and you can actually destroy a practice. "A successful dental practice is a small group of individuals and you have to do all the things effectively so that everyone can be happy. You have to care for each other like the extended family that you are. We all pitch in when someone falters and support them until they are back to full speed and realize at some point you may need to be supported yourself".

Ever the perfectionist, Rhys works hard to communicate with his lab. Photography is used for his laboratory to achieve an excellent result. "There are such subtleties to this whole process. Photography is the key to transferring those subtleties to the laboratory to get the exquisite results. You have to be an excellent photographer to get the excellent photograph. Ultimate success is built on sequential steps, all performed at an unwavering level of quality that can't be missed or short changed.

Practices that try to do aesthetics without photography are not giving the patients the results they could give."

Rhys candidly says, "over the years, most of the patients have said 'no.' In the first few years of aesthetics, the closure rate was 5-10%. Now, we have had some months where it has been over 90% as people are coming in pre-selected from marketing or referrals. They arrive knowing more; it is not uncommon now at the initial appointment to close the case and collect the fee. We recently met a patient on Tuesday morning desiring a better smile for her upcoming wedding about six weeks away. At that time we did a direct composite mock-up to show her what we could possible do. She returned for complete records on Wednesday afternoon (radiographs, models, photographs, definitive treatment plan and consents) and paid the fee. I did a diagnostic wax-up that night and we prepared 10 minimal prep ceramic veneers and provisionalized her case. We left for a planned vacation that afternoon and seated the case a few weeks later well ahead of the wedding. She was thrilled. The moral of the story is you make hay while the sun is shining, but to do that you all have to be prepared and willing".

Up until recently, the majority of cases took two years to significant treatment. Now, no one walks in totally unprepared. "It has to do with how much they think they know about you before they come in. Now, when someone says 'no,' my attitude is 'not right now.' 'No' is an emotional decision; very changeable. Circumstances change; it can become a 'yes.'" Rhys' advice is to always be gracious in accepting their decision as it is their right.

Though it appears easy in the Spoor world, Rhys says, "I examine my overhead and make adjustments where possible. Some overhead cannot be cut; raising your fees is the alternative. Maximizing profitability is a balancing acts of fees, procedures and time as well as knowing your marketplace. On comprehensive cases on a new patient, they do not have anything to judge on; there is more latitude here. You want to have a fee structure designed to provide optimal care with flexibility to redo as the patient desires, as this is going to happen."

"What we do is so emotionally based, you can have a perfectly sound clinical and technical case which is a 'failure.' A patient can be greatly influenced by what others say, especially if it is a friend or relative. One negative comment can and does set off a cascade of events that ultimately may result in replacing much if not all of the recently placed work. A recent example involved a case where the patient was perfectly satisfied with her result until a co-worker thought her teeth looked gray. The patient previously lived with severe tetracycline stained teeth and was indeed hypersensitive to the shade. Even though the patient approved the color of her teeth several times during the process, she was now dissatisfied. If you want to have "the customer is always right" type of service, your fees have to support the occasionally redo of a case. You also have to remember that patient satisfaction is the biggest key to long term growth and success of an aesthetic practice."

Rhys' grandfather's advice for career was dentistry as he observed the dentist had respect, control of his income and time for vacations. While Rhys was in graduate school at the University of Washington, the funding for his master's thesis in fisheries was cut by the federal government. He remembered his grandfather's advice, did a 180 degree turn (literally, dentistry was across the street) and feels now it was the best decision he could have made as it has been a terrific career.

Not a planner as a young person, Rhys started in a friend's empty office space with "a chair, some instruments and an attitude." Finding it "a bit slow," he associated for a year and purchased a practice in Ballard, with marine repair and building as the main industries in this blue-collar part of Seattle. The retiring dentist had practiced 24 years and 90 days in the year of purchase. In three years, Rhys tripled the production working 200 days. He had become insurance-free, converted an operatory to a photography studio and had a 24-hour Smile Channel in his reception area covering the shared parking lot of several restaurants in the evening.

"As I studied aesthetics with Dr. David Baird (a very enjoyable and eye-opening experience) of Bellevue, WA and sought the council of Bill Blatchford (great systems and solid concepts), I realized I had reached my full potential in Ballard. To do the kinds of dentistry I wanted, I needed a downtown location and in 1996, sold my Ballard practice purchasing a downtown practice doing $800K a year in 190 days. I thought the practice would be a good base for transition. What I realized later, I really purchased the location. It turned out to be an insurance-based general practice and within two years of purchase, I had less than 20% of the original patients. I actually had to rejoin Delta to hang on to the patients that were in the practice I purchased."

The essence: Collection is the same as production and is collected before the time of service with few exceptions. 130 clinical days, eight hours per day. Ten to twelve new consults per month taking at least an hour, complimentary. Closure rate around 60%.

Rhys and his team see all marketing as important to get potential patients to inquire. But the internal marketing, like how they are answered on the phone, email or text get them through the door. "It's about being nice and treating people like family; being honest and making the client always right. People can see when you are really focused on them and giving your best. They will tell others." Team Spoor's goal is to have no or minimal discomfort, both physical or psychological. Painless local anesthetic techniques, sedation if necessary and keeping the guest truly comfortable through the process is Spoor internal marketing.

Dr. Spoor spends significant amounts on external marketing (8-10%) and they have tried almost everything. They have an excellent website, www.rhysspoor.com and steer everyone to their website which is always evolving. Rhys' advice on external marketing:

- Develop yourself as a brand
- Select a delivery medium and be consistent
- Study what others are successfully doing in your area.
- If no one is doing anything, start with the least expensive and easiest.
- Be first or different, be consistent and patient

- Market to your market
- Make marketing match you—-hard to be a veneer practice with 80% kids.

Continuing education is the basis of a successful and fulfilling practice. "Many of the procedures I do on a daily basis didn't even exist when I started in practice 33 years ago. The rate of change seems to be increasing and those that don't stay engaged through continuing education will fall behind, plus it makes practicing a lot more fun."

About his courses, (see www.rhysspoor.com for information and schedules), Rhys says "many of the doctors tell us our courses are some of the best, if not the best of any continuing education they have ever taken. I take great personal satisfaction in getting those kinds of reviews. Our process shows the doctor how to comfortably and predictably create a great looking and functioning smile. We talk about how to do it in a timely manner, minimize the complexities and difficulties and probably most importantly, how to psychologically carry the patient from desire to result. And they have a great time doing it."

Rhys is a natural teacher and loves sharing with others. "I enjoy the interaction with people and seeing them grasp new ideas, seeing that little light bulb come on in their heads, realizing they have control over their destiny and they are truly artists who can add value to society. Once they see themselves that way, their patients see them in that light, too. I enjoy being a part of that."

"I tried to be successful from the day I started. I had a high desire to follow three rules:

- #1 Be honest
- #2 Do the right thing
- #3 Do your best

Rule #1 is pretty black and white, honesty is the best policy.

Rule #2 requires defining what is the right thing when it comes to dentistry. The right thing is what is correct for you as the dentist and what is best for the patient. Only you and the patient can decide this. No one else was there. Always put care before commerce and treat patients like they are your family. The intrusion of the dental insurance industry has distorted the doctor patient relationship and puts commerce before care. Rule #3 requires a commitment of time and money to continuing education. Being successful is an attitude followed by actions that support that attitude. You have a lot of control as to where your career will go and it starts right now."

www.rhysspoor.com

Dentistry can give you so many options and you have the ability to choose any or all of those options. The wonderful part of being a dental professional is it gives you the opportunity to truly help other people while allowing you to control your time and environment so you can pursue other passions for a fulfilling life.

Dr. Rhys Spoor

Business Decisions: A Cosmetic Transformation

Location and community composition are important in the success of a cosmetic practice. Because cosmetics is optional treatment, the success ratio is lower and it takes more marketing to specific people of value to continue success. Dr. Spoor was in a solid part of Seattle and knew to be highly niched, he needed to move uptown. He purchased a general practice in an excellent location. Much focus and hard work were needed to transform to a strictly cosmetic practice.

Achieving a successful cosmetic practice has become the dream goal of the American dentist. In moving toward that goal, there are real decisions and consequences which will be felt economically. Every general dentist would love to believe he either possesses or is rapidly moving towards a practice of cosmetics. As we all know, there is a huge gaposis between having "veneers" listed in your Yellow Page ad and the reality of presenting and performing the artistry to which every dentist aspires.

Are you and your practice financial and emotional candidates for a successful conversion to cosmetics? Can one mix cosmetics with TMJ, implants and pedodontics and become known in your community for aesthetic choices? What is the financial impact of moving from a general practice to a cosmetic, restorative practice? These are serious questions to contemplate in today's rapidly changing dental marketplace and the financial impact of those choices can be great.

Cosmetic dentistry is now one of the many discretionary items our patients can choose to purchase. We are competing with many other goods and services so we must have a clear and excellent reputation. Seventy-two million boomers want to look good, feel good and last a long time. It is not a given that a beautiful smile is even on the boomer's 'want list.' Patients are at choice here, too.

Choice is the operative word here. There are many choices, each creating a different economic consequence.

Step One. The first and most important area of choice is creating a solid vision of what you want your dream cosmetic practice to look like, financial results, reputation in the community, extent of cosmetic skills, etc. Practice vision is a personal extension of who you are as a dentist. What are your important standards and values in life? A strong vision demonstrates itself in every move you make as a dentist. Your actions speak your vision.

When a solid vision is articulated, it is very motivating for yourself and staff to see a dream picture of the future without barriers of time and money. You must have a clear picture of the end result. Otherwise, needless motion and money is wasted in making sideways decisions. You must stand for something strong or you become a meaningless victim of every fad. In Proverbs, it says, "The people without vision will perish." This vision will be tested continually by you, your staff, patients and other dentists.

Why cosmetics? Are you prepared to have a community reputation of high fees, catering to a select clientele and possible loss of former patients who only want to continue to do what their insurance covers?

One of the reasons you selected dentistry was to make a difference in people's lives. Be clear and strong in defining why you want to be a cosmetic dentist as the success of this exercise will greatly influence your cosmetic results. Your vision and action will show how committed you are to having a cosmetic practice. Your vision must be well defined and be a burning passion for you.

Step Two. Another business choice in the path to a cosmetic practice is the important technical skill courses. One weekend veneer class does not a cosmetic dentist make. Excellent clinicians, the "dentist's dentist," offer on-going hands-on courses to be on the leading edge of cosmetic artistry. This is an ongoing process. Continue to take courses from the best. Expect to spend time and money in acquiring the skills and reputation necessary to be known as an excellent cosmetic dentist. Demonstrate your commitment by becoming an accredited member of the AACD.

Take the high road on these courses and become the best of the best. You owe it to yourself, your patients and your dental peers to do the very best cosmetic work possible.

Step Three. Another huge choice on the path towards a cosmetic practice is to have your own mouth completely restored to today's standards. Select one of the top Doctors and expect to pay for it. How can you present cosmetics if don't see the value for yourself? Your staff also must have the most beautiful smiles. This is a great opportunity to listen and handle your own objections as well as your staff concerns. Objections might be, "no time, don't NEED it, what will it look like?" If you cannot show value for your staff to have cosmetics at little charge, how do your presentation skills rate in working with your patients objections.

There are many advantages to a cosmetic update and one is it demonstrates to yourself your level of commitment to cosmetics. Your staff and patients will notice with much mutual admiration and motivation exchanged. You set the pace for your office. I so admire dentists who "walk their talk."

Step Four. Another choice is for you to define cosmetic dentistry as well as define how extensive cosmetic and restorative treatment will be in your practice. Some Doctors will be dabblers, some desire a 50% mix and others are looking at a pure cosmetic and restorative practice, perhaps in conjunction with other appearance specialists of plastic surgeons and orthodontists in a boutique or spa setting. All are choices. It is very possible to change the nature of some practices from a general practice towards a cosmetic practice in 36 months. If a general practice is large with too many patients, a strong cosmetic practice can result in 24 months. If a general practice is small and not financially strong, a pleasing cosmetic practice will not be the result or it will be a most difficult road.

If you see a strong cosmetic practice in your future, are you currently offering and presenting cosmetic treatment? If you have an advanced skill level in cosmetic technique and cosmetics still represent less than 30% of your practice, ask yourself one more question—why? It is one thing to have learned excellent technical skills but if you and your team have not mastered the presentation skills in asking needs development questions and really listening to patients, your cosmetic skill will remain academic and indeed, a dream.

Questions 5 through 9 are for you to determine the present financial strength of your practice. In moving towards more comprehensive treatment, some of your general patients will leave your practice. A small practice, deeply in debt, cannot handle that potential financial dip. Cosmetics is not the Great White Hope. It will not bail out a bad practice.

In moving towards a cosmetic practice, choices are made eliminating some services as endodontics, periodontics and referring these to specialists. However, before eliminating services, you must add and increase cosmetic services or your income will definitely drop. Tom Peters in *Thriving on Chaos* mentions when the overhead is high, it is difficult to impossible to make changes. If there is a healthy margin of 40-45% profit, change is easier (general to cosmetic). In other words, dentists need to have their practice in order before making drastic changes.

You may have too many patients at present and can afford to eliminate some by dropping insurance and eliminating services other than cosmetics. If you learn to present cosmetics, the nature of your practice can quickly change.

Cosmetic Practice Potential For Success

	Present	36 Months
1. % of cosmetic income	_____	_____
2. % of overhead	_____	_____
3. % of collection from insurance	_____	_____
4. % of staff expenses	_____	_____
5. % of laboratory expenses	_____	_____
6. Practice debt	_____	_____
7. Personal debt	_____	_____
8. Retirement Investment	_____	_____
9. Age	_____	_____
10. Cash at end of month	_____	_____

Step Five. Just Do It! The best way to build a cosmetic practice within a general practice is to just do it. Decide to what extent you want to be known as a cosmetic dentist and let the world know. By having your own work done by the best, you become excited and motivated to continue. Do your staff's cosmetic dentistry. Have before and after picture albums in every room with framed pictures in the reception area. Dr. Spoor sends a strong message of cosmetic enthusiasm and skill to his patients in his reception room by showing framed after pictures of his patient's beautiful smiles. Dr. Spoor also has a photo studio in his consult room demonstrating to patients his emphasis, competency and commitment to appearance artistry.

Use the very best dental labs with the possibility of three to four day turn around for special clients. Eventually talk with every patient about the possibility of more long term care, looking good and avoiding problems. Ask questions and keep asking questions.

A cosmetic dental practice is about choices. Your patients also have the opportunity to choose. How would your patients even know you do great cosmetic work? What is the reputation you have in the community? Are you known for anything special? How committed are you and your staff to breaking out of the paradigms of the old dental model and creating something new called a cosmetic practice? You are always at choice and there are economic consequences to each choice. Which do you choose and how committed are you to making it happen well?

Bill Blatchford, DDS

From the Blatchford Play Book: Courage to Succeed

When things are not going as you planned, it does take persistence, courage, focus and commitment to succeed. Dr. Spoor has used much energy, focus and hard work to have a highly niched cosmetic practice.

- ➤ Easy to be ordinary, takes courage to excel
- ➤ Takes courage to stand by your convictions
- ➤ Takes courage to keep fighting when you are losing
- ➤ Takes courage to stick to your game plan and the unrelenting pursuit of your goal when you encounter obstacles
- ➤ Takes courage to push yourself to places you have never been before, to break through barriers.
- ➤ We are here to be tested, to be challenged with adversity, to see what we can accomplish
- ➤ Takes courage to look deep within your soul
- ➤ Courage is not how a person stands or falls, but how they get back up again
- ➤ All glory comes from daring to begin
- ➤ We cannot discover new oceans unless we have the courage to lose sight of the shore
- ➤ There is no substitute for 'guts'
- ➤ JFK said, "the stories of past courage can define that ingredient— they can teach, they can offer hope, they can provide inspiration. But they cannot supply courage itself. For each man must look into his own soul."
- ➤ Winston Churchill said, "Courage is the first of human qualities because it is the quality which guarantees all the others."

18

PURCHASING A PRACTICE

Dr. Chris Mueller

Dr. Mueller is a very young-looking dentist producing $1M only four years out of dental school. (Now $1.7M and 15 years out of dental school.) He is smart, personable and definitely not slick. The most important thing in Chris' life is his family. He wants to be successful yet the three practice opportunities and decisions really "just happened" and he was in the right place at the right time.

He is surprised to find himself in the company of profitable dentists. "One of the reasons you may have selected me is that I was able to do between two to three times my production without significant overhead increases due to sound management principles and acquiring a patient base large enough to allow block booking plus minor fee increases."

To be near their families, Chris and his wife selected Port Orchard. It is a working town in Washington's Puget Sound, supplying labor for Bremerton Navy Shipyards and now becoming a growing bedroom ferry commute to Seattle.

Chris says, "I graduated in 2001 from the University of Washington and there are still moments when I am not 100% sure I will be successful. I purchased a practice that produced $250K the year of purchase, choosing it over another practice producing $600K. My decision was largely based on personal meditation and was against what logic would have dictated. Starting out was very intimidating and success was far from assured—I couldn't even get a bank loan, eventually having to ask my father for the $180K purchase price."

This practice had produced $450K. The owner was a skilled practitioner who had several personal issues preventing his full time attention for the last several years. He had walked away in Oct. 2001 leaving his two staff to keep it running without his input. Chris was able to work there two days a week for seven months and keep the practice open. He became attached to the small, comfortable setting. His first goal upon purchase was to return it to the historical production, reintroduce a hygiene program and eventually grow to $600K.

"Before Blatchford coaching, we had collected $433K on $480K production for the first year and I felt we had reached a comfortable level and life was going smoothly. In Nov. of 2003, the dentist across the street unexpectedly passed away and life got complicated again. I was absolutely sure I wanted nothing to do with his practice and tried to convince a friend of mine to purchase. Weeks passed and Bill Blatchford heard of my possibility. How could I, a relative rookie, handle the patient load of two mature dentists? I worked slower so it seemed logical that I couldn't produce more than I was currently doing, let alone the production of two faster dentists. It seemed overwhelming—not to mention the pending staff issues, having to move offices, paper work headaches, etc. There were times where I firmly decided it would be too much work and chose not to rock the boat. Finally after much consultation, I put my hat in the ring. By this time, five months had passed. The daughter of the deceased doctor felt I was the one her father would have wanted and chose me. His practice had collected $450K in 2003. The selling price was $260K for the practice and $250K for the building. I hoped to at least bring my production up to my $600K goal."

In retrospect, he feels definitely "the best business decision I made was buying the second practice and having Bill help me manage it. I never thought I would be this successful this early on." Chris was 33 years old.

The second practice challenges included the deceased dentist's wife being office manager and running the business on a peg board system with several helpers. She died six months before her husband.

Other pitfalls on the path to excellence for Chris include:

"Holding on to staff too long once it was apparent they weren't sharing your vision. I kept hoping they would suddenly change, thinking, 'we can make this work.' If you have to MAKE it work, then you are spending energy instead of becoming profitable. I can't emphasize this one enough—by lacking the courage to make uncomfortable choices, I limited the heights to which we could rise. Once these choices were made, it was like cutting a hot air balloon free from its moorings. The interesting thing is that I knew in my gut that everyone of these people was not going to work out but my mind kept hoping they would change. People may change but not very much."

"In the same vein, avoiding difficult situations for long periods of time by occupying myself with less important tasks. Technically, this is probably called 'risk avoidance.' It's much easier to tinker with a faulty handpiece than to have a frank discussion with your receptionist about how you're not happy with her performance. Essentially I had subconscious procrastination in the tough areas which just prolonged the problem."

"Thinking busy was being profitable, this is coming more clearly to me as I have to write off large amounts of accounts receivable from bad accounts. I treated patients with the notion we'd get the money someday and I'd rather stay busy than not. In retrospect, I should have had a staff meeting, gone home early or read a book."

"Not having a clue what the receptionist was doing and assuming she was doing what I envisioned regarding AR management, scheduling, recall, etc. I found out this was not the case most of the time. I was too busy with teeth and home life to actually check on it. I also did not know the computer system like she did and felt I could not match her experience. The solution was to purchase a new system where we were on equal footing. I should have had weekly meetings to discuss the numbers from the start."

Trying to save pennies on supplies. Chris graduated from dental school with $15K debt by scrimping plus marrying a wife with a steady job after his freshman year. He is mindful of money.

On the other hand, Dr. Mueller's practice highlights have been "purchasing his first practice, purchasing the second practice, acquiring a team that supports my vision and is loyal to me while implementing techniques learned from Dr. Blatchford."

At the merger, Chris brought two full time staff plus one part time hygienist and he inherited four full time staff. Staffs were less than enthusiastic in joining together and making changes. In fact, "at the first staff seminar, the groups began forming 'camps' and would team up on me. It wasn't long before most departed or were shown the door. With that mess behind me, I realized what a burden I had really been dealing with every day, and only later did I realize the real effect it had on my physical health. Carrying this kind of stress has untold negative consequences."

In 2004, Dr. Mueller and newly reorganized team collected $797K, besting his goal of $600K. He had between three and seven staff the year he combined practices. Overhead was 71%. In 2005, his production/collection finished at $1.1M and overhead of 51%. His team is four full-time staff. Currently, they are attracting 30 new patients a month and working 170 days. In his first practice, a crown was $796. Currently, it is $1250.

Moving into a five op., fifty-year-old building with the last remodel in 1971 was not the most fun. Because the dentist had not moved out, there was thirty years of dental junk. Chris found equipment he had no idea it's function. The first phase of remodel was to be paint and carpet but evolved to renovating the welcome area, larger hygiene rooms and lighting, new door with Chris' logo, new floors and more. Phase 2 was the three doctor operatories. "It began to feel like I was an established dentist rather than a new guy in someone else's office."

Chris had signed with a management consulting firm prior to Bill but they were "unable to motivate me to make any of the tough choices—firing staff members, etc. They still use me as a reference and I tell them to call Bill."

Chris feels Dr. Spoor's anterior courses "really changed the way I practice and enable me to offer treatment I had never considered before." When Chris purchased his second practice, he started addressing periodontal disease in the hygiene department, offering posterior bonded ceramic restorations, promoting veneers and referring time consuming extractions. "Some in my area cannot afford optional care or aren't interested but I know they will not say 'yes' until I ask."

He and his team are all involved in sales. Now that they have met all the patients, they are role-playing with receptionist asking questions on the phone, hygienist doing an excellent job of asking questions and setting Dr. Mueller up for the details."

"When we are playing our 'A' game, the day flows by without hardly noticing—all of a sudden, it is 5 PM. You're happy and your dinner conversation is not about work. You feel good about the services you have provided and your patients express that as well. You do not dread going back to work after the weekend."

"My staff is really motivated by the Blatchford bonus. The first one was just a couple hundred dollars, then the first one over $1000 really got them moving. Now anything below $3000/monthly cycle is disappointing to them. They have more ownership of the practice now. My vision statement also has helped motivate them. We read the statement monthly and dedicate the first part of the meeting to finding areas we are need to improve. There is power in having a written statement outlining in detail your office philosophy. The biggest struggle along the profitability path for Chris has been staffing. "Finding a group around me who respected me as a dentist and a person and really saw my vision of what we stood for and where we are going has by far been the hardest part. If you are honest with yourself, you know deep down if someone is the right fit or not. I have learned you need to trust yourself in these matters and not let your fears rule you. Now, Chris feels his leadership allowed him to create a vision statement. The team with the vision tends to address the issues themselves. "I do provide the final word but often times, I don't need to. Don't get me wrong—we still have plenty of room for improvement."

The next biggest struggle for Chris was feeling he did not have enough patients or accepted treatment to block book effectively. "To be honest, we were scared to try it and never did. We let fear keep us from knowing if it would work. This was solved by acquiring another practice which gave us enough patients."

Internally, Chris and team started asking for referrals tried to secure as many patients of the former dentist as possible by providing superior customer service and quality dentistry. I try to make anesthesia as painless as possible to generate word of mouth. We take pictures of our larger cases to display."

Externally, "we offered free whitening with Valpak and received a handful of quality patients but most just came for the free whitening.

The bulk of our growth had been acquiring older practices and securing the charts from a third office. It is much easier for me and available in my community."

Chris was always a voracious reader and this helped him to perform well in school. Thus he was able to study whatever he wanted in school and go to the dental school of his choice. He was originally a marine biology major. During his junior year, he did a semester at Hopkins Marine Station in Monterey, CA. He loved what he was doing but "Clinton was slashing government spending on research and many post-docs were hanging around looking for work. I didn't want to go to that much school and not be guaranteed a job in the end. Many of my classmates were pre-dent and pre-med. I didn't want medicine so dentistry it was."

During undergrad, Chris served two years on a mission to Zurich which gave him insight into what he wanted from life. He chose a wife to be a great partner and support. He sought advice from those who had done this before and found Bill Blatchford through them. "I didn't know what life would bring but I feel this has laid the foundation upon which success has followed."

What has happened since 2005:

What I have learned in the decade since then is that goals that are written down and reviewed really happen. We have been steadily increasing growth each year and at the same time gradually taking more time off. I recently found my Blatchford folder from an early Dynamo meeting and happily noted that all but one of the goals I set at that meeting have been met.

During the recession of 2008, we noticed the cosmetic cases dropping from around a case or two per month to a couple of cases per year. For years, I had been hearing fellow Blatchford doctors talk about placing implants but couldn't picture myself following suit as I didn't enjoy surgery and would do anything possible to avoid laying a flap. I couldn't imagine using a bur the size of an acrylic bur in the mouth. After considerable encouragement, I made the decision to take a course. During the first course I placed my first implant and I haven't looked back. Having taken further surgery courses, I now feel this is my favorite procedure, not to mention the most profitable. Having these cases to fill block appointments offset the loss of cosmetic cases and we didn't see a dip in production or collection during the recession. I felt very fortunate when hearing fellow dentists discuss the economic downturn in their offices. I added a CT scan a few years ago and I can't imagine practicing without it—whereas a few years ago I couldn't have imagined practicing with it.

At a Peak Performance meeting, fellow Blatchford Doc Kim Okamura encouraged me to get Invisalign trained, another area I didn't see myself embracing. Again, after taking the first course and many additional ones, I have really enjoyed adding ortho. After adding this in 2011 we have used it to take us to the next level. At that same meeting Steve Greenman got us hooked up in treating Sleep Apnea. It is another area that has broadened our ability to benefit our patient's lives. I doubt any of these services would have been part of my practice without my association with the other Blatchford doctors.

This brings me to the next big change in our practice. For years since the original book, our daily production goal was $7600. We got really good at nailing it and feeling good about it. After a few years we set it to $8400 and we made it again routinely but it never felt easy and often we scrambled to fill our blocks. At the last Dynamo this spring 2016, my team made the decision to go for $10,500. I felt like we were reaching to hit $8400, no way we could do it. But there is power in having a goal to book to and in the following six months we have averaged over $10,500. We are set to have another record year of $1.7M on 170 days, 55% overhead. This year we have added another assistant to handle the load and another day of hygiene but we still have only a FT staff of four. I just like the small office philosophy with fewer people, and much less drama.

Having sufficient income combined with time away from the office has afforded me freedom. I reached my goal to be entirely debt free before age 40. Not having to worry about finances has given me the greatest gift of time to be with my family as my children grow up. This year I have been able to spend five memorable weeks so far on family vacations where we created memories that I will always cherish. As my oldest twins are now sophomores in high school it is becoming all too apparent how fleeting this time together is and I am so grateful to have the ability to have this time while we are all together still.

chrismueller@hotmail.com

Mueller family. A masterful feat to take a picture.
Thanks Dad, for being home more.

Mueller family in the Swiss Alps.

The Mathematics of Cosmetics — Multiplying Your Opportunity

Dr. Mueller is the prime example of taking advantage of several local practice sales and incorporating them into a $1M practice by the time he was 33 years old. Purchasing an existing practice is a guaranteed way to multiply your opportunities. Are you looking for that opportunity in your community?

How to increase your practice, that is the question. Most practices have the capacity and technical skill to produce much more which would dramatically increase the net. We want to increase the number of fee-for-service patients who sees value in a new smile. We need more non-media generated and non-coupon generated patients. As technical skills increase, so should production.

In many practices, new patient numbers are changing. The old fee-for-service insurance model offering practices a steady flow of newly insured patients for their free six month cleaning and exam may no longer be in the majority in your area. Alternative delivery systems of managed care initially are attracting those patient numbers. This has created a concern for private care practices who have the technical skill to deliver much more excellent dentistry.

In a strong general practice, healthy new patient numbers should approach 15 to 20 adults a month. When the focus of the practice is to present every patient with ideal treatment, a 50% case acceptance rate can be achieved if verbal skills of doctor and staff are excellent. This number of new patients will result in $500,000 to $600,000 gross production.

If your new patient numbers have reached a plateau in the last several years as your ability to deliver cosmetic and better dentistry has increased, you have cause for concern. There are several solid answers to the concern over declining new patient numbers. One solution is to create a program of niche marketing. This is deciding the direction of your practice, building a reputation within that niche (cosmetics, reconstruction, mercury-free, etc.) which will garner new patients who see value in your excellent care. A marketing budget should be established and a professional marketing expert should be hired who understands niche marketing and the desired reputation for your practice.

The second solution is to purchase an existing practice in your area and merge it with your present practice to create the potential of an excellent strong practice. The benefits to patients, the selling doctor and your bottom line are very positive if the purchase is structured correctly with a win/win for all. A practice merger is a perfect opportunity to create a new image in niche marketing with a dental marketing expert.

In fact, marketing with a practice acquisition is a must.

One win is for the patients of the purchased practice. With warm welcome letters and increased verbal skills of staff, the patient retention is high. Patients feel well served. The new energy level is high and newer technology might be offered. The selling doctor wins when the financial structure of the sale supports his goals and is able to move onto his next project. The new doctor wins when the contract structures the sale so there is financial reward from the beginning. He must be in control and able to see benefits from the beginning rather than strictly a payback for the first five years Avoid costly pitfalls in purchases and sales by having a coach who represents you.

Another benefit to the buying doctor is these patients are already established patients who see value in regular dental care. It takes more effort and funds to attract new patients than to geometrically reproduce established patients. A practice merger brings established patients.

A successful practice purchase really requires the help of a smart practice broker. His goal is a win/win for both parties. We coach our doctors to avoid the heartbreaking pitfalls of practice purchase with strong guidelines. A few are:

- Purchasing the practice outright and avoid any "partnership" situation

- Seller leaves the practice with a non-compete covenant

- Purchase price is definite at time of sale
- 100% financing through a bank as a total buyout is the best.

	Your Practice	New Practice	Combined
Prod.	$400,000	$250,000	$650,000
Staff	$80,000 (20%)	$50,000 (20%)	$130,000 (20%)
Lab	$40,000 (10%)	$25,000 (10%)	$65,000 (10%)
Supplies	$20,000	$12,500	$32,500
Rent	$40,000	(Close office, pay rent for 6-12 mo)	$40,000
Equip	$40,000	(Sell or donate to charity)	$40,000
Misc	$60,000	$60,000	$60,000
Total	$280,000	$87,500	$367,500
Net	$120,000		$282,500

The ADA average overhead is 73%.

NET AFTER PAYMENT $232,600

FINANCING　　　　$250,000 New Practice Production
　　　　　　　　　$200,000 Estimated cost

Nothing Down with 100% financing. Finance for five years at 10% Annual payment is $50,000 prior to taxes.

There are practices for sale within a five-mile radius of your office which could nicely merge with your existing practice and satisfy the new patient craving. Some of these practices are smaller and are overlooked by recent graduates as they perceive they could not make a living on just that practice.

Practices may be for sale because the doctor is going back to graduate school, has family needs in a different area or feels it is just "time to sell." Some practices may be listed with a broker while others are not officially for sale. This is where networking with your peers works well as there are dentists who are either frustrated with the present system, nearing retirement age or perceive a different practice environment would be best but have not definitely made a decision yet. By lunching with possible candidates, you can offer your support should the decision be made. Be first in line.

Almost all practices can qualify as eligible for a cosmetic transition. If the seller was an adequate dentist with a loyal following, it is very possible for you to have a high patient retention rate and after several hygiene cycles, to see the fruits of your communication skills create good results. If the seller has a small high end cosmetic practice where most work is completed, this practice has value for you, too, as the reputation is already established and these patients see value in cosmetic work. They will continue to refer their family and friends to you.

With a desired result of 10 to 15 adult new patients a month, a practice merger is a great solution. Depending on the patient base, new patient flow can increase from 10% to 50%. There are several important keys to having the results show well:

- Use a smart broker representing the buyer (you)
- Develop strong relationships with patient so treatment is not perceived as overwhelming
- Learn and master skills in communication and enrollment
- Broker represents the one paying the fee

I have seen excellent cosmetic practices produce incredible work on five or less new patients a month. What this means is that doctor and team have learned how to form lasting, trusting relationships and have mastered sales skills which create value with the patient. Without these sales skills, your excellent technical cosmetic work will unlikely be in someone's mouth. Therefore, purchasing a practice and doubling your new patient flow is not the whole answer. You must be able to convert those new patients into dental missionaries for your cosmetic work.

Once the practice purchase has been made, your "new patient" flow has been increased to meet your goals. The next immediate step is learning and mastering new skills in enrollment to make certain these new patients are asked questions to discover their needs, really listened to as never before and treatment is actually completed. This then is the real value of purchasing a practice. Do you and your staff have the excellent skills necessary in today's market to present and have accepted ideal treatment?

Bill Blatchford, DDS

From the Blatchford Play Book:
Pre-Game Preparation

Dr. Mueller is the coach for their morning huddle where all team members are present. Here are some points to make that meeting effective.

► Morning huddle run by the coach

► Team arrives early, focused and finished with breakfast

► Who is ready to play?

► Who knows the score today?

► How will best service be delivered today?

► Start huddle on a positive note, welcoming your team for another good day

► Scheduling blocks are set to goal

► Whole team starts at the same time

► Team has copy of today's schedule in hand

► Select referral requests, long-range planning conversations with recare guests

► No personal talk during huddle, focus on serving guests well

► Doctor starts at 8 AM with one great "A" patient

► People notes on guests are shared so all know current information

► Team is playing their 'A' game today

► Coach asks and receives team commitment to make and exceed goal next four days

► Complete huddle five minutes before first guest

► High fives all around

19

RELATIONSHIP BUILDING

Dr. Curtis Chan

Curtis is successful in San Diego for many reasons and one he shared is his ability to connect with people. His physician father was in private practice, then in emergency room medicine (as he was fed up with insurance and never seeing his family). When Curtis was 13 years old, his father joined the US Air Force. The family lived in Germany for five years and continued moving. Curtis feels this forced him to make friends quickly, to connect with everyone on some level and he accepted this as a personal challenge to build relationships.

"Being raised in different cultures forced me to hone my natural skills in relationship building. I became a good listener. At our practice, we exude caring and connect with people. We feel 99% of sales is building those relationships."

He has mastered these skills well enough that it basically serves as his marketing program. He virtually has no formal external marketing program and still attracts 20-25 new patients a month, mostly from happy client referrals. "Getting out into the community and serving others has helped me become friends with hundreds of people. Building trust with these relationships continues to be a key ingredient for why my practice continues to grow year after year."

None of the following Curtis does is part of his marketing program for his practice, yet these are skills and beliefs he personally holds: 29th year member of the La Jolla Symphony as a cello player, accomplished pianist, very active member of his Christian church and weekly host to a couples Bible study on marriage building, and a member of a very large well networked family in San Diego. Curtis co-chairs the San Diego Dental Golf Group and the Seacoast Christian Golf Club. His wife, Mae, heads up several outreach ministries at church: Women's Outreach, Mothers Of Preschoolers (MOPS), Children's Ministry, and an Adoption Support Group.

Curtis is the fourth of five boys, all involved in the healthcare field. Four are dentists and one is an optometrist. When Curtis joined the Blatchford program 23 years ago, he wrote three goals: to get out of debt, to get married, and to live on a golf course. All of course have come true and the very best of all of these, was finding Mae and getting married at 36. They have two natural children (Michelle and Jonathan), and have adopted two children from China; Grace and Matthew. Now as teenagers, they all attend a Christian private school as they are being molded into becoming leaders of tomorrow.

How do five boys all enter the healthcare field? Curtis' father was one of four brothers and two sisters orphaned in British Guyana, an English settlement. Their aunt was a Seventh Day Adventist and she urged them to emigrate to the U.S. All were high-achievers as the sisters became nurses and three of the boys went to medical school in California. The "cool" youngest uncle dropped out his second year of med school and later entered dental school at Loma Linda where he went on to specialized in orthodontics, greatly admired by the five nephews.

When the elder Dr. Chan joined the Air Force and was stationed in Germany for five years, one of his sons mastered the German language and graduated No. 1 at his dental school in Universität Tübingen, near Stuttgart. In the father's 23 years of service time, he served in the First

Gulf War and was a commander of the largest mobile US Air Force hospital in Ryad, Saudi Arabia.

Mae, Curtis' wife, has an interesting family journey to the U.S. When the Chinese Revolution was occurring after WWII, her grandparents fled mainland China to Korea. With nine children, they eventually came to the U.S. Two of Mae's aunts are dentists. Her father is a chemist who immigrated to Japan. In 1957, when he was 18 years old, he came to Abilene, Texas to study at Hardin-Simmons University.

All five Chan boys are high achievers. Clayton is the neuromuscular expert and has his own dental teaching institute in Las Vegas. He is an accountant by training and then a dental lab tech. He worked for Kerr as a dental lab tech and developed shade guides for composites along with a chemist and a physicist. After two children, he graduated from Loma Linda School of Dentistry and began his search for the "elements of occlusion." He was still not convinced of the Pankey occlusal direction. He was searching for an answer and found Myotronics. He became a passionate advocate and according to Curtis, "couldn't sleep and even gave up surfing."

Curtis decided by his junior year in high school to be a dentist so he "could help people improve their health." He had always been successful in setting goals and being the best he could be in school, in cello or piano. He feels success is not about money, for that will come.

In an associate position, he did hygiene during the week and some dentistry on weekends. Eventually there was a Del Mar practice for sale but Curtis had already invested in a new car and home. The practice was six months behind in rent and had 200 charts. A local dentist helped him put the financing together. He continued as an associate as he built his practice. He had to clear $4500 a month to break even.

In his fourth year, his brother Clayton graduated and they needed to start working more hours. They found a better location to share office space. They followed the Pride model of 'Bigger is Better' with 1.5 assistants per operatory, two hygienists and two in front. "I knew I was digging a big hole." Clayton had a Blatchford cassette tape and Curtis felt "it just couldn't be true." Eventually he heard Bill at an evening program. "I needed to do this but I felt badly doing something different than my brother."

"I arrived with eight staff and one by one, they excused themselves." Gradually he selected people who could see his vision and others came back, some driving 1-2 hours to work with him and the team. "All the things Bill said made sense and we moved to new levels. The 'right-sizing' took two years, while building with the right staff and systems. As we improved, we weeded out the low end of patients and created opportunities for better patients to find us. Bill also encouraged me to discover what I liked to do, thus I dropped endo, amalgams and most children."

The hardest thing Curtis has done in dentistry was to make the change to refine his practice. "I just had to jump in and do this. It was a 90 degree turn from the direction we were headed and it was tough." On the other hand, "doing Blatchford was the best thing I ever did. He became my mentor in dental business, made me accountable and is a good coach. I had a dental practice that was 'running me,' rather than 'me running my own practice.' I had tried many dental management programs, but the information that I received only worked for a few months, and then I was still back where I started. What I was searching for was a program that would give me lasting results. A program that would teach me how to create successful systems in my dental office to be more efficient. I needed to learn the skills to be a good leader. The Blatchford program gave me all of this plus much more. Their personal coaching program, helped me realized my potential and additionally helped me realize that all my dreams were attainable. We set goals and established a "New Vision" for my dental practice. Within a year, I started to see results. As I become a better leader and wiser business-man, I was able to realize and experience my dreams and goals. I began to have control over my time and finances. Now I love going to work every day, and enjoy helping all my patients. It's fun creating value for what we do by being effective communicators. It's a joy to provide the best dentistry can offer. This program helped me redefined who I was as a dentist, and steered me onto the highway of success!"

Curtis' dental team continues to be fired up as they are high ($1.5M production/collection) achieving office. They choose the days and weeks they want to work. And the team gets plenty of "time off with pay." His team works hard at refining all their systems, improving on communication styles, and supporting each and every day. They enjoy the benefits of being a true Fee for Service office that is not dependent on dental insurance.

Curtis' style of leadership is to find key people who are leaders and give them the latitude of making decisions. The leader's clear vision guides them and this eliminates the micro-managing. Regular communication is key with a focused morning huddle, weekly staff meetings, evening meetings and BMW 4x4 which is four hours every four weeks set aside for training and mastering conversations and systems. One of his mottos he continually reminds his team members is that "we are on a journey and we must continue to improve ourselves daily."

www.curtischandds.com

Dr. Curtis Chan

The five Chan boys, 1964

The five Chan boys, 1996. Four dentists and one optometrist

Col. Claude Chan, MD (Curtis' dad)

Dr. Curtis Chan with family

Mints on the Pillow, Bugs in the Bed

Dr. Curtis Chan has a stellar reputation. He is known for kindness, service, and excellence. His guests return and new clients arrive because of positive buzz in the community and personal networking. The continual challenge is to serve your guests to the highest standards at every moment. As the great sales trainer Brian Tracey says, "Everything counts, and everything counts."

Hold a victory celebration when you complete treatment on a guest and your conversations are focused, listening is keen, timeliness is observed, finances work, and the guest is overjoyed with the technical results. Do you take time to recount all the "everythings" that allowed this guest to be ecstatic? Do your systems ensure every time your guests visit, your treatment will go smoothly? Do you have qualified staff members who understand each system? Do your staff members sing your praises and the reasons they are happy to be working in your office?

Patients depart because of unfulfilled expectations, usually in the administrative area. It's the bugs in the bed that create ruffled feathers, not the technical work. Our systems of communication and follow-up are critical.

An office culture can develop haphazardly. With little direction or distinction, staff members do what they did in other offices. We remain average. With each staff member working independently, we miss opportunities for great conversations with patients, guests slip through the cracks, and we achieve excellence in a random manner. Strong systems form a practice culture when the leader is clear and communicates the bigger picture. Great staffs are drawn to clearly communicated passion and share the vision. Deep thought, clarity, and communication are the keys to invigorating your staff and being accountable. Where are the bugs in your bed that patients will notice?

- **Timeliness** — Unfulfilled promises of time. Running late is a symptom of a lack of direction from the leader. Are you Dr. Everything to everybody?

- **The waiting game** — Guests who have accepted treatment wait and wait for the doctor to appear, while they observe a flurry of activity elsewhere. Pareto's law of 80/20 indicates 80 percent of your profit comes from 20 percent of your patients. Do you know who they are and is their visit filled with exceptional care?

- **Random scheduling** — This creates chaos, little production, and an emotional void by the end of the day. Learn block scheduling and schedule each day the same. Schedule to a daily goal by knowing your overhead per hour. Make that a figure to exceed.

- **The insurance game** — If you leave the patient out of the insurance loop, you make your office the center of insurance knowledge. Instead, collect upfront for most patients and give them the insurance form to submit for reimbursement. Quit creating work and trouble for yourself.

- **Order-taking** — Your first question to your patients should not be, "What is your biggest concern?" If it is, your diagnosis and treatment result in "small-picture" items. In the sales world, this makes you an "order-taker," rather than a creator of opportunity. Learn modern sales skills and begin with, "How may I help you? How would you like your smile to look in 20 years?" The result of order-taking is your patient's assumption that your treatment mix is limited and "if I want to beautify at 55, I should seek that care elsewhere."

- **Promises, promises** — When you say you will do something, do it! Connect with patients and staff. Excellent communication with your lab and specialists and networking in your community all lead to excellent results. Do you have solid systems in place to keep promises?

- **Layered staff** — A common "bug in the bed" complaint I hear from airplane seatmates is, "I seldom see the doctor, because the staff does all the work." Consider using skilled treatment coordinators who see the guest through to a happy completion. "It's not my job" is a bug in the bed. Hygienists should know all fees, assistants should know the schedule and how to do complete financial arrangements, and the doctor should know how to handle patient phone calls. What systems do you need to implement to make sure you clearly hear your patients and they feel complete and special?

Mints on the pillows are wonderful, yet momentary. Bugs in the bed are stories that are repeated to friends and family in the community. Solid systems will eliminate the bugs. Is it time to get some help...or do you want to continue to be average?

Bill Blatchford, DDS

Blatchford Game Plan: Playing your 'A' Game

Dr. Chan works at being a good coach for his team. Relying on internal marketing as he does, the team must be playing their 'A' game at all times.

During the final games of the NBA playoffs series several years ago, the Los Angeles Lakers lost very few games. However, after one particular loss, Shaquille O'Neal shared his simple explanation that "we didn't bring our 'A' game. We have an 'A' game but we didn't play it tonight. We played our 'B' game, instead. We're bringing our 'A' game next time."

The L.A. Lakers benefited greatly that year from excellent, strong coaching. Phil Jackson took already talented individuals and honed them into a focused, lean and mean team to deliver results. A good coach, who is passionate about the game, plus already-skilled players who come together to play the "A" game, result in a winning combination.

What is your "A" game in the business of dentistry? Do you and your team know the game plan and come prepared to play hard all day, every day? Like the Lakers, a dental staff (including the Dr.) must arrive with all the up-to-date skills, sharp focus, mental balance and passion to deliver the best.

Tiger Woods, in his stunning win of the US Open, shared that he played his "A" game all week. He demonstrated skills, unbelievable focus, passion and practice with his coach, which resulted in a record win. He also spent five important hours practicing on Wednesday before the Open. Tiger Woods practices! If we were as good as Tiger, would we practice for five hours on routine skills?

What is Tiger's "A" game? How can a dental office play an "A" game like Shaq? The cheese has moved in dentistry and the need is great to reinvent ourselves. Instead of playing the old routine and thinking small, we must create an "A" game.

What has changed in dentistry? There has been a virtual clinical revolution with new products and techniques. This creates the possibility to deliver exceptional service and results, thus branding yourself in the marketplace as special and different. Dentistry has become truly optional and dentists who play their 'A' game, believe they are in the elective health care field. Patients also have become more sophisticated, realizing they do not NEED our services, but choose to have a more beautiful smile that works well and lasts a long time.

Another important aspect of change in dentistry is the people part of the 'A' game. For years, dentistry has been a product-driven industry. We are a service industry and are evaluated by the public by our level and focus of service. An 'A' practice sees dentistry as a people game and hires staff who genuinely enjoy people.

To play the 'A' game, the players, including the doctor, need to present themselves with the highest skills possible. Taking the latest, greatest courses like the Kois Center for Excellence, becoming accredited with American Academy of Cosmetic Dentistry or a national equivalent and continuing to reach for the next level is an important part of the "A" game.

An attitude of curiosity on the part of all players must become part of your practice culture. An "A" team has a sense of curiosity about life, others and the workings of things. At work the curious man finds an opportunity to learn while he earns. Having mastered the often routine requirements of the job, his curiosity demands more, seeking answers to questions raised not by others but by his own desire to know. At play, myriads of questions bombard the mind. Every aspect of existence stimulates a question to the curious man. It is this drive to know everything, this drive that sustains the curious mind. Strange to say, the satisfaction is not the answer, but in the search itself. Be curious and hire curious people.

What is the game plan for implementing this curiosity and skill? It takes action to make your dream plan a reality. A vision in your head is dead. You must dig deep inside to discover your "hot buttons" and inner passion for excellence and making a difference for others. You must be able to communicate that picture to an already talented team. They must see what you see with possibly even more intensity.

The "A" game plan must include practicing of learned business and communication skills. Just because you have been in dentistry for twenty years does not mean you have developed the listening skills to allow a patient to dream. Learn the skills and practice asking questions, then really listen.

An "A" game must include reading of books on business, sales and marketing. What is your current book to put you in the "A" game? Audio and videotapes are available for stimulation. Phil Jackson of the Lakers has selected philosophy books of required reading for his talented team.

Be curious to the point of taking classes seemingly unrelated to the field of dentistry. Classes could be on self-esteem, psychology, web design and graphic artistry, stocks and financial planning as well as a physically demanding class. How does this connect to the "A" game? A person who has stretched to learn new ideas and skills is a much more enthusiastic person with others. Enthusiasm is the basis for sharing dreams and creating value for others.

An "A" game is one of constant improvement. Don't accept the status quo. Turn your weakness into a strength by practicing to constantly improve. Do not accept that your numbers have stopped growing and you have reached a plateau. The 'A' team reinvents themselves and breaks out of the doldrums.

Select a coach who pushes you. The coach can see things from a different point of view. Metaphorically, you are inside of your own leadership box and the instructions for getting out of the box are written on the outside. A coach has to be able to see what is happening, because you can't. The 'A' team finds a solid coach.

All these are skills and attitude to develop on your own time and bring your "new" person to the office team. At the office, the "A" game is being on time, creating dreams with patients and delivering excellence.

A highly skilled, mentally focused team is thinking positive thoughts, complimenting each other's work, seeing the big picture with a vengeance, self-starters (including the dentist) and real team players who boost each other and patients. They are excited about today, tomorrow and possibilities. Their dreams are coming true.

Everyone likes to think they play an "A" game because they are tired at night. When the Lakers lost, they were really tired and had given 110%. A checklist for the "B" game would be a practice culture of micromanaging, not so silent complaining, relying on reasons—not results, stars with little teamwork, a lack of curiosity and reliance on the status quo.

We all have a choice in the matter. Put on your game face and play your "A" game. Make the "A" game your practice culture.

Bill Blatchford, DDS

From the Blatchford Playbook: Game of Life

A balance is what we are after. Dr. Chan and his wife Mae have a happy family life, an active spiritual being, are givers in the community of life and his practice supports all this.

► Keep on playing the game

► Never retire and hide; you are needed somewhere

► What is your plan for a meaningful retirement?

► Never deprive someone of hope. It might be all they have

► Dentistry supports your life; life comes first

► Develop passion in life

► Be interested in others

► Be curious about your surroundings

► Always play full throttle, live each day

► Say "yes" to opportunities even when you do not know the outcome

► Demonstrate happiness

► Enthusiasm is contagious

20

FLOURISHING IN THE DESERT

Dr. Samir Patel

Dr. Patel just started the Blatchford Coaching Program and he already is on fire. He has a very profitable practice in an area of great need. Yet, he was working 200 days a year with a 90-minute drive each way from his family.

Samir's wife, Hetal, is a physician and needed to have a three-year residency match in Arkansas, but Arkansas did not accept Samir's dental credentials. He needed a place to support his family and found an associateship in Thayer, Missouri. His initial attitude was "I can stick this out for three years." After a year, he was offered the purchase and now finds Thayer a generous adventure.

Thayer has a population of 1500 and a drawing area of 50 plus miles. Besides a neighboring dentist, the closest others are 30 miles in either direction.

Samir found Blatchford through John Weyland's IV course (IVwisdom.com) where five other Blatchford dentists were a positive force. Samir arrived at the Blatchford door saying, "I want what they have."

Samir was born in London and came to Atlanta at age five. He was asthmatic so played inside with model planes and worked with his hands. After he graduated from the Medical College of Georgia, he worked in a fee for service practice and then two years of corporate.

Hatel was born in Zambia and when her family came to the U.S., they worked at motels. Two of the four children became physicians. Samir and Hatel built a large home in Jonesboro for their extended families. They have two small children and want them to have experiences but avoid being spoiled or undereducated. They are working with them on high morals and principles.

Dr. Patel feels Blatchford Coaching has taken a lot of stress away for he and his team. He is now working 132 days with a goal of $19K a day with implants, dentures, and extractions. Before Blatchford, he was doing $165K a month. His first Blatchford month was 13 days for $200K and a second month of $200K in 11 days. He dropped Medicaid in that period. Samir upped his deserve level and increased his fees from the 40th percentile to 70th percentile. It is a blue collar, very rural area and the median income for a family is $30K. There is high unemployment, railroad workers, riverboat operators, with many retired and elderly over 60 years. He just started dentures last year and has increased his denture fees.

He has taken over $100K in CE in the last 18 months. His reputation is the best technology and the cheapest dentist. He is the only dentist in Oregon County, with 10K population. It is not a real desirable place to live, yet, there are several nurse practitioners in the area. Several of the dentists do simple dentistry. Samir is the only one doing implants and wisdom teeth, and is just starting sleep apnea.

Blatchford's Block Booking helped them be much more organized. He likes a morning block with a big implant case. Before Blatchford, he would make an extra trip on Saturday to do treatment because they had difficulty scheduling (that happens when staff is paid by the hour).

At first, his team was hesitant but it didn't take long for them to become engaged and excited. They are doing 11-day cycles and the first cycle, there was a bonus of $1100 each. Before this all started, he gave his team members a raise as their pay was so low. In the second cycle, the individual bonus was $1500 each.

Dr. Patel feels they can produce $3M. He feels next year, he will be producing $2.7M. He thinks back on dentistry before Blatchford and he was getting steroid shots in his neck and taking a mild muscle relaxant every night. He takes Bill's motto to heart: "If it doesn't add value to your life, get rid of it." Dr. Patel told Bill, "I am only three months into the program and feel I already have my money's worth."

www.thayerdentalclinic.com

Samir and Hetel Patel

The Patel family

Blatchford Game Plan: Dental Math

Dr. Patel needed a place to practice for three years while his wife did a physician's residency in Arkansas. He found an associateship with a 90-minute drive each way in an area of need. Considered an under served and undesirable area, Samir has turned this practice into lemonade. Making the numbers work successfully in your dental practice is not a skill taught in dental training. The business of dentistry eludes dentists and they end up on a treadmill, running faster and faster, never able to catch the economic relief of which they dream.

Without returning to school to acquire a Master's Degree in Business, you, too, can learn to watch your numbers and make them grow in the direction you want. The result will be more joy in practicing and you can fall in love again with dentistry.

When you uncover how much it costs to deliver dentistry in your present mode, you can then make choices about the direction you want to pursue. You can change the mix of treatment presented and the manner in which it is delivered to produce.

Most practices schedule what ever treatment needs to be completed. There is no design or thought to cost per hour or overhead. If you could design your day so that your overhead is lower than present time and your treatment delivery was increased, would you be interested in making a change?

In this study of dental math, we are going to focus on the mix of treatment delivered and how it is delivered. In examining the mix of treatment, we are looking at three categories. We will label these "classes." This is not the technical diagnosis of treatment classes but rather a determination for dental math. The "class" we are discussing here has a monetary value. We are examining the money of the practice because it is a business and we want our business to work well.

Our three "classes" are defined in economic return. Class I are procedures that total $125 and under, Class II are procedures which total $126 to $300 and Class III are procedures that total over $301.

Why? The average dental office overhead per hour is around $250 per hour,** plus lab. With two providers (one dentist and a hygienist), overhead per provider is $125 per hour. No one else has studied your practice in this way to actually discover how you are spending your precious time and great skill.

** *Producing $500K with a 75% overhead and a lab bill of $7500, your monthly expenses are $30K a month and working 120 hours reached an overhead per hour of $250.*

Make a study of your appointment book for the last ninety days. Use Exhibit A as your study sheet. Reviewing your last three months of appointments, find the number of hours in your office that have Class I procedures done and what percentage of the total time is spent in Class I.

Do the same with Class II and Class III. With a $250 an hour overhead, the average dental practice spends 75% of time doing Class I procedures which you will note, does not cover the overhead. 75% of the time! No wonder you feel you are working hard but not producing much.

EXHIBIT A
Ninety Day Study

	Hours spent	% of Total Time
Total number of hours _____		
Class I ($125 and under)	_____	_____
Class II ($126 to $300)	_____	_____
Class III ($301 and up)	_____	_____

The average dental practice spends 10% of time doing Class II procedures which is producing just enough to pay the overhead. In the average practice, only 15% of the time is spent producing procedures which total $301 or more.

What is the message and how can we make a change? Our goal is to flip the percentages around so that 75% of your time is spent producing procedures that are $301 and above and only 15% of your time on procedures that produce $125 and under per hour.

The difference between a practice producing $30,000 a month and $80,000 a month is the mix of treatment. An $80,000 a month practice is spending 75% of the time doing procedures $250 and over and 10% of their time doing procedures under their overhead.

What are the steps that need to be taken to make this happen in your practice? First, you must believe that your practice is not average. What is average? Are you an average dentist or an outstanding dentist? Do you desire a practice of distinction or an average practice? Are patients attracted to you because you are average? I think not!

Determine what procedures you do that would be $301 and over. Are you doing one crown at a time (the worst one) or is there a possibility the diagnosis and presentation could have been multiple units saving the patient time and emergency situations? How much longer does it take to do two units as opposed to one?

Before you completely reject this idea of multiple units because we might be doing "unnecessary treatment," let's consider some possibilities. Time is the most important commodity today to our patients. They do not like to spend time in the dental chair and they definitely do not like to have three to four appointments for procedures. Looking at the bigger picture for the patient, what value would there be for the patient to have you, the expert, see if there is other work to be done that could prevent multiple appointment and dental chair time in the future?

The second step is to create with your patients a long term treatment plan based on the three universal desires to look good, feel good and last a long time. With a long term treatment plan based on what the patient wants, you begin to step out of the "patch" club and into more comprehensive dentistry.

Diagnosing multiple units requires some skill building with your staff. Since looking good is one of the primary goals of patients, we need to learn to ask questions which bring out the values and desires of the patients. See Exhibit B for some possible questions staff and doctor could ask. Showing pictures of beautiful smiles is a visual stimulation and addresses the patient question of "What will it look like?"

EXHIBIT B

What would you like your smile to be like in 20 years?

What do you like best about your smile?

Looking at these pictures, is there anything you would like to improve about your smile?

What do you like best about the appearance of your teeth?

Whose smile do you most admire?

The next step in changing the mix of treatment is to examine your fees. Are your fees average or even below average? Studies show people purchase items because they desire them and see value in owning that item. Price, contrary to dental belief, is not the major factor 90% of the time. If your work and skill is above average, charge above average fees.

The next step which will allow a different mix of treatment is to block book your schedule. We want to develop an extraordinary reputation of service in our community. We want to deliver our excellent dentistry is a comfortable, non-hurried atmosphere. By block booking, you produce 80% of your daily goal by lunch. Block booking means you see only 2-3 patients in the morning, doing multiple units on each patient. Hold those blocks of time open to take care of the needs and wants of your patients.

When you have completed your appointment book study for the last 90 days and find the percentage of time spent on procedures, you will want to make changes. Change is difficult, yet, if your desire is to have a dream practice where patients see value in the excellent dentistry you have to offer and there is joy for you and your staff, change is necessary. You cannot keep doing things the way you have always done them and expect to achieve a different result.

Hopefully, this dental math is a real eye-opener for you and your staff. An awareness and belief in you is the first step. You can turn the numbers around in Class I, Class II and Class III. Dental math does make a difference.

Bill Blatchford, DDS

From the Blatchford Play Book:
Playing Your 'A' Game

► Team is present and focused, no outside distractions or worries

► Guest is number one priority

► Team is on time

► Doctor is technically skilled and can deliver quality

► Guest drives the conversation when asked open ended questions

► Staff listens as guest talks 80% of time, sharing their thoughts

► No matter the direction of conversation, staff allows guest to feel heard and important

► During treatment, guest has all creature comforts

► Assistant and doctor are symbiotic in procedures, organization and preparation. There is a quiet confidence and all is well

► Guest is overwhelmed with the results, thinks the temps are just right

► Guest thinks whole team are magicians and walk on water, refers many

► Team gifts guest with fishing magazine subscription and delivers gift basket of local products to his work

► To quote Brian Tracy "Everything counts, everything counts, everything counts"

► Systems are in place to assure success in procedures, no reap points to retake impressions or lab work not at office on time.

21

REJUVENATION

Dr. Jeff Hadley

A happy ray of sunshine in Sin City is Jeff. Dr. Hadley came to us at age 50 concerned about his debt and wanting a long-term plan to retire. He had a nice background for success with degree from USC Dental School and a GPR at Great Lakes Naval Hospital. He has been in the Navy Reserves for 20 years. Thanks for your service, Jeff.

Another important part of his success is his Spanish-speaking mission to Uruguay as a member of the LDS. One does not associate Las Vegas with Latter-Day Saints but it actually is a strong community in Henderson, NV. He is active in his Church and he and wife, Jennifer are looking forward to adult missions. There is also a large Spanish speaking community in Las Vegas.

What Dr. Hadley is so pleased with because of Blatchford, he is out of debt. He loves being out of debt. He can look back to see his debt did not allow him to be free. Now that he is out of debt, he is very cautious about making new purchases or investing. Another plus of being debt free is, he became a fly fisherman again, something he used to do a lot but felt he did not have the freedom of time.

Looming retirement and taking care of his family with a practice debt was a big burden for Jeff to carry. He loves dentistry and wants to work as long as possible. Paying off his practice loan was huge and now putting away those monies for retirement has brought him such peace. "I have hope and a fighting chance with much less debt than before the Blatchford plan." Their retirement includes lots of travel, several Church missions, and a beach house with room enough for several grandkids.

He has reinvented himself as a leader through Blatchford. In dental school, he thought leadership would be easy as he is a people person. This epiphany of leadership has caused the whole complexion of the practice to change. He decided to be a leader and he felt confident when Blatchford lays out the plays and recipes. He moved forward and now expects more from himself.

He recognizes accountability is hard. He knew he needed someone to pull him forward. Jeff said, "if you have a decision to make which you perceive is painful or hard, you keep procrastinating and the opportunity will soon evaporate. You lower your standards into your own comfort zone saying "I'm OK, I can get by. I'm OK with this number."

They now take 13 weeks off and the team is off, also. One person rotates through for phone and office attention. Team comes back from time away rejuvenated and ready to go. They can see they need time away about every five weeks.

He is still "married" to insurance, down to six relationships from many. He dropped those insurances which would not honor a materials upgrade. The team and Doctor work at not being a slave to insurance so their conversations are as if insurance is not a factor.

Dr. Hadley loves implants and is on a path to his Mastership in the AGD, so implant courses are at the top of his list for continuing education. He feels his team is well trained in patient conversations. He is also into sleep apnea, using a medical biller and participates in AADSM. He has used a direct mailer, social media and their website.

He has a home sleep study device which the team is committed to a patient a week taking it home.

Thus, this team bonuses between $1800 and $280 each. This bonus period, they earned $335 each. His daily office collection goal is $8500. His bonus to himself is to stay physically fit and to that end, he is training for a marathon. His goal is to continue to "see his feet" and keep his belt at the same loop. Being out of debt has freed his time to be healthy.

As a Naval Reservist, Jeff is deeply patriotic. In 2006 with an active practice, he was activated and deployed to Naval Hospital Yokosuka, Japan. "It was a great honor and privilege to leave my practice and family to serve the men and women of our country. It was a very small contribution compared to what others have given. It was the reason I have stayed in the Reserves and the reason we train." Jeff hopes to make the 30-year mark in the Naval Reserves.

Jeff said he will miss the starting of school as all three of his daughters have completed high school. They once celebrated the first day of school with a Father's Prayer and a big sendoff. Morgan is earning a degree in interior design and started her own walk-in closet and kitchen pantry design business. Blair is married, an esthetician and hubby is a new policeman for City of Henderson. Meredith has three part time jobs as she prepares to start BYU in January. Now they are empty nesters and Jeff is not ready to be there.

Las Vegas is a community of change. Areas emerge and deteriorate quickly. There is a transient feeling in Las Vegas. His leased office is in an area which has gone downhill and he is looking for another space when his lease expires.

Dr. Sunshine is grateful to Dr. Christina Blatchford and Dr. Bill Blatchford for having a program which allows dentists to be more profitable and get rid of debt.

www.smilesbydrhadley.com

Blatchford Game Plan: Exit Right 4 U

When dentists become skilled working with new materials and techniques, often they feel a rebirth and rejuvenation about their profession. They can't believe how much more enjoyable practice is again. When a dentist keeps up with current education, there are ways to continue the enjoyment as well as the income stream from dentistry. Dr. Jeff Hadley is one who got a "shot in the arm" and feels great about continuing to practice.

More than 31% of solo practicing dentists today are 55 years or older. Since most dentists have traditionally retired between 60 and 69, retirement is a "hot" topic. Financial advisors feel you will need around 70% to 90% of your current net in retirement. Yet, the baby boomers (now mid 50's to 70's) have reinvented each phase of their lives, never matching what has been customary. What will retirement be like for the boomers? What will be right for you?

Goal setters who have planned for retirement since the beginning have accumulated five times what a non-planner has saved. An ADA survey indicates dentists save 10.6% of their income which is below the federal limit of 15% contributions to a qualified pension fund.

The average dental net in 2001 was $173K. In retirement planning, eighty percent of that is $138,400 which is $11,500 a month. If you retire at age 60 and live another thirty years, your need would be $4.1 million from interest and savings.

The figures are staggering for the slightly unprepared. What are the choices for the today's boomer dentist? Sale? Partnership? Associateship? Practice in a different way?

A sale is worth about 18 months to two years of net income which is then taxed for capital gains and deprecation. Although this will seem like a simple statement, you must be aware that a sale is final. You are now no longer a dentist in that location. There is no going back. The book is closed.

Partnerships in retirement have their own sets of pros and cons. By reviewing again the motivating factors for entering the profession, you may find independence and freedom on your list. Selling half your practice to an unknown partner means you have surrendered your freedom and half your net income in exchange for about nine months of net income. The staff will still look to you for leadership and details.

Becoming an associate after thirty years of private practice could be successful, if you have the qualities to be an employee. Will you be happy doing dentistry for someone else? Do you have the qualities to be a team player under someone else's leadership and rules?

Continuing to practice in a different manner is a viable alternative. You can continue to feel needed and serve others on your own terms. We call it "Retire As You Go," and the absolute to making this work is that you enjoy dentistry. This is a program for the optimist, the eager and the bright. This is for doctors who want to learn the latest thing and continue to be involved.

There are some real advantages to keeping your practice viable. Presently, if you have a $1M practice, you are able to deduct about $50K of expenses which include a leased car, continuing education travel, entertainment and other. Upon selling your practice, these after tax expenses are now yours. Another big advantage is the psychology of your earned status in the community.

Why not take advantage of the qualities which drew you to dentistry in the first place? These might be independence, freedom from outside control, leading your own destiny and money, especially if you did not accumulate a bundle.

You design your ideal practice days, plan your continuing education around travel adventures and attract a staff to work your schedule. You may want to work three days a week for three weeks and take the fourth week off. If you can continue to work on your own terms, netting $150K and not having to use your retirement funds until you choose, count the advantages and your blessings.

It is true; the value of your practice may decrease. Weigh this; if you can continue to practice another 10 to 15 years, making $1.5M, against the original final selling price of 18 months net. I have a number of excellent boomer dentists who are reinventing "retirement" under their own terms. Are you interested in being one of them?

Dentistry offers the greatest possibilities for choices, even in retirement. If you enjoy dentistry and want to continue feeling needed and wanted, consider "Retiring As You Go."

Bill Blatchford, DDS

From the Blatchford Play Book: Overtime

Of the 100+ plays in a football game, only four or five plays make a real difference. The challenge is that you do not know which play will make the "win." Dr. Hadley and team play full out.

► Develop your sales skills

► Shift your paradigm from education to listening

► Shift from NEEDS to WANTS

► Develop relationships by being interested

► Ask questions to uncover wants

► Ask deeper questions

► Only present solutions when you have asked many questions about their dreams and desires

► Write scripts for asking questions

► Practice, practice, practice

► Vince Lombardi says "every game is decided on one or two plays"

► Play every play as though it is the one

► Learn from your mistakes, don't repeat them

22

THE BREADWINNING PARTNER

Dr. Tracy Davis

Tracy is married, mother of four and one of two owners of a $4M general dental practice. She, too, is part of the Big Switch where the female is the breadwinner and husband, Matt, who is well trained in business, is the house-husband and busy father running these four children to all their activities and keeping up with his many other roles.

Dr. Davis is actually the first in her family to go to college. Since then, her sister, several nieces and a few cousins have taken the mantle. Though she was a biochemistry major, she thought medical research in a lab would be her niche. She didn't care for hospital setting so switched to research at the university. Here, she met Dr. Bibie Chronwall, a dental school instructor, who encouraged her to find herself. Her husband, Matt, was encouraging her to go to dental school. She was seven years out of college and applied to dental school.

Three years out of dental school, they had four children under four, including a set of twins. Tracy said their marriage "went dark" with the demands of four under four and two diverging careers. She and Matt decided to grow together instead of apart to make the best decisions for their family. They decided Tracy should stay with dentistry and Matt would do freelance work. He has an MBA and degrees in computer technology and accounting, which is extremely helpful to the dental office. He juggles kid logistics into his business roles.

After ten years in Kansas City, Tracy is back with her extended family. She and Matt really work at fitting in. She is aware they have more time off and more funds available. She admits it can be tricky. She remembers the Bible verse of Luke 12:48 "from everyone who has given much, much will be demanded." Her mom is 76 and Tracy hopes the siblings can work as a team to make her mom's life easier and care for her needs. She tried to give back to everyone around her. Her fondest "giving back" moment for dentistry is changing the smile and outlook of a 15-year-old with amelogenesis imperfecta by placing 28 crowns, pro bono. Her goal is to give away 10% of her production during the year and tracks this monthly. (No, this doesn't include insurance write-offs!)

With all her weeks off, many are stay-cations with the kids in school. They all ski, love the beaches and the Disney communities are well known to the Davis family.

In dental school, a classmate had said, "you should meet my dentist." It turned out to be the practice where she became an associate with Drs. Marc and Kelly Barnett, a couple who had done very well and were thinking of eventually retiring from active practice..The details of her associateship and buy-in were clearly stated before she began, and the team immediately saw her as a partner, which eased the transition when she did eventually change from associate to business partner two and a half years later Then, four years ago, Nick Matthews (one lucky dentist fresh from dental school) became a partner. A year after this juncture, Tracy and Nick hired Blatchford Solutions to make sure they could continue this incredible journey as the original partners stayed for another year before retiring.

The area south of Springfield is growing as a suburb yet, there are still open areas. Springfield is the home of Missouri State, at 25K students. Schools are good and they love their children growing up with many cousins and family.

Tracy has completed half the John Kois curriculum, thanks to Blatchford, she says. Her partner Nick is interested in surgery and sinus lifts and is taking Frank Spears courses. Tracy and Nick both took Arun Garg's implant continuums They provide sleep apnea treatment and their goal is ten patients a month into appliances. Tracy feels there is a huge opportunity to treat sleep apnea in their area.

The whole office goal is $24K a day with $10K for each doctor. They have four assistants, four hygienists and three receptionists. They are providers for Delta as it reaches over 50% of their patients. They are rid of all other insurances.

Dr. Nick Matthews and she share a very small office together and they talk every day. Communication is key. Karen is a wonderful practice administrator who helps to keep things moving forward and helps them both with project follow through. Tracy and Nick share similar values and frequently spend time together outside the office with their families. They each have their strengths, recognize this, and use it to the advantage of their office.

The team's monthly bonus is steadily rising and is currently around $400 for each team member. Their team is motivated with more "ownership mentality" because of Blatchford systems in place.

Their office implemented AM and PM huddles that helps the entire team prepare for the patients and keep the team on the same page. Communication is key. During a four-hour meeting every four weeks (4X4), the team role plays scenarios, learns new procedures, participates in a discussion and application of a book all have read, as well as housekeeping items such as complying with the ever-changing HIPPA and OSHA regulations. They do a fun team-builder event outside the office each quarter.

Blatchford Solutions has really helped her personally have more balance in her life between her family and business. She enjoys her extra six weeks off with her family. Her team is all rowing in the same direction and it is a positive environment. She is encouraged to be a better dentist and is learning more dental procedures through great CE and is rejuvenated with the field. Connecting with other Blatchford doctors has proven to be very beneficial. This allows her to see how others have solved similar issues that come up, such as dealing with ever-changing insurance plans to seeing others ideal schedule blocks to helping with a clinical case to getting feedback on materials and CE and more—basically inspiring her to raise her own bar of excellence. She is thankful that Dr. Bill and Carolyn Blatchford took the time to set down with them a full day discussing vision and goals for their family as well as the business. Starting with "why" has made all the difference in their "what" and "how."

www.exceldental.com

Blatchford Game Plan:
Five Star Service Scheduling

The successful private practice must be known for serving patients well. The goal of this 'on-time' practice is to stand for excellent service. Patients will perceive outstanding service when appointments are fewer and more treatment is completed at each visit. Outstanding service in the patient's eyes is their perception they are the only patient and full attention is paid to their needs.

This Five Star Scheduling greatly benefits the busy dental patient. Reluctance on the patient's part to accept larger treatment stems from the old method of scheduling multiple patients in a triple booking schedule. A single crown took two-and-one-half appointments from their busy lives. They perceive a whole quadrant would take ten appointments. "Let me think about this, Doc,' is usually the response.

Holding large blocks of time open in the morning for longer and more demanding treatment creates a boutique practice, a practice of choice. If you had a two hour, three hour or four hour block of time and no other operative patients, how much treatment could be completed? What would be the benefits to the patient? The patient, who has accepted treatment receives individual attention, unrushed and focused. The doctor doesn't wear rollerblades in trying to see three other patients at the same time. The dental office is elegantly quiet and the doctor can focus on technical excellence. The staff loves this scheduling because each relationship is stronger with Five Star Service Scheduling.

What benefits are there for the practice? Five Star Scheduling creates an opening for larger diagnosis and acceptance with immediate treatment. When a doctor is so busy with smaller appointments, the subconscious does not want to diagnose a large case. If the patient accepted, the patient would have to be literally squeezed into an already exhausting schedule. The doctor then places this patient into the "Watch and Wait" Club. With larger diagnosis and acceptance, the production per hour increases, matching and even exceeding the overhead per hour, which increases the net return to the practitioner. Wow!

The Five Star Service Schedule is further enhanced by evaluating the most productive procedures and scheduling those patients in the morning blocks. To help evaluate your most productive work, the doctor and receptionist can do a 90-day study of the practice.

First, determine the overhead per hour in your practice. Eliminate the items which are legal to deduct but do not directly impact a practice—a leased car, continuing education/vacation, etc. Determine the true overhead per hour of the operation.

If the overhead in a practice grossing $500,000 a year is 75% (ADA statistics for average overhead), the overhead is then $30,000 a month, divided by 15 working days is $2000 of overhead per day. The daily overhead is divided into 8 hours and $250 an hour is the overhead.

We will use this figure of overhead.

Review the appointment books starting three months ago to present. You will be marking each hour in Class I, Class II, or Class III. The following chart will help in your discovery if your overhead is $250 per hour.

- Class I appointment is any hour spent producing from No charge to $200.

- Class II appointment is any hour spent producing from $200 to $300.

- Class III appointment is any hour spent producing $300 and over.

Ninety days is enough time to see trends developing. What you will find is a vast majority of time spent producing work under overhead, which are the Class I appointments. These are the smaller appointments, which eat into productive time. In many practices, 75% of time is spent producing work which does not even pay for overhead. A noteworthy portion of the 75% are Class II potential procedures which are squeezed and mashed into a triple booking arena which creates multiple short appointments for procedures which should take one hour when treated as a solo patient.

What percentage of your time was spent in Class III appointments? If the Class III patient had been the only patient (no triple booking), what could the income per hour have been? If, during this 90 day study, Class II procedures were booked simultaneously with other patient's treatment, how much extra time was spent to accomplish the Class III procedures? What would have been the total time of treatment if that patient were the only patient being treated?

If you are spending 75% of time on Class I appointments and 15% of your time on Class II appointments, the challenge for the future security of this practice is to change the mix of treatment and the manner in which the treatment is scheduled.

The goal of Five Star Scheduling is:

1. Take care of patient's needs by being aware of their time, diagnosing lifetime dentistry and working from that plan.

2. Achieving a daily production goal by deciding in advance what the production goal is and schedule accordingly.

3. Provide a stress-free environment which means staying on time, completing treatment scheduled, no interruptions and having a pattern to each day.

Say "Goodbye" to multiple patients being scheduled simultaneously for treatment, which does not cover overhead. Rather than filling every line in the appointment book, Five Star Service Scheduling refers to a planned day which is actually repeated every day where blocks of time are held for larger and more optional treatment. Develop a template for perfect scheduling which allows the patient maximum time with the doctor, fewer and well-planned appointments, being seen on time and released on time while receiving the smile of their dreams.

Rather than having the dentist see many patients each day and do a little on each patient, we are going to start to serve patients well by seeing fewer patients while doing more treatment on each patient. We are going to be creating value for appearance and longevity rather than patching and doing one crown at a time.

Five Star Scheduling is easy to institute and has a great result for the patient. In the morning and every morning, the doctor sees no more than three patients. We have reserved a two-hour block from 8AM to 10 AM and two one-hour blocks from 10AM to noon. Notice even though we have more than one operatory, we book only one chair. Remember, this is a Class III patient and they definitely deserve their time of excellence. Surgeons do not make house calls during scheduled operations.

By changing the mix of treatment and how it is scheduled, we serve our patients well. Increasing the percentage of time spent doing Class III procedures where the practice is actually exceeding the overhead creates a situation of financial compensation. By block booking, the morning schedule facilitates 80% of the daily production goal. The doctor can sit with one patient and feel fine about it. The running days are over.

Five Star Service continues in the afternoon. Right after lunch, two co-diagnosis appointments are held for new patients returning after their initial cleaning and exam last week or it can be a recall patient to whom you are now speaking with about a long-term treatment plan.

From 1:30 to 3:00 in the afternoon, we have scheduled shorter appointments when your patients need a single surface filling, a quick check, suture removal, etc. This is also the only time emergency patients are seen. Five Star Service means declining an emergency patient if the only time they can be seen is during productive Class III time. As you start to speak to your patients about more long-term care, your emergency demands diminish. During this aerobic stretch in dentistry, your motto is "Start, Finish, Stop" as opposed to "Start, Stop, Start, Stop, Start, Finish." In other words, even in shorter procedures, sit down and complete that patient before moving on.

Our Five Star Service Scheduling allows you to complete the day by seating the same number of units prepared in the morning. Patients look forward to this appointment so it is a relaxed, happy celebration of completed work, rather than squeezed between three patients. You have time to celebrate the beautiful final product by having your laboratory tech visit or taking final pictures. Patients love the attention.

Block booking creates an impression of excellent service to your patients. They feel they are receiving the best treatment from the best office when their needs are met with timeliness. Block booking is very simple but it does take effort and commitment to change from your present system. Do not change any appointed patients. In your appointment book, draw a line when you are no longer solidly booked. Design a template of blocks and what treatment you want in the blocks.

Commit yourself to making it happen. Change your mix of treatment from 75% of Class I to 50% of Class III appointments. Encourage your staff to speak optimistically about the opportunity for individual attention from the doctor when you and he are fresh in the morning. Work on effective scheduling with scripting like:

> "Congratulations! Your new smile is going to look great. This is Dr. Blatchford's favorite thing to do. To maximize your time and have the doctor when he is fresh we reserve time in the morning for these types of procedures. You will be the doctor's only patient during that time. We have time at 8AM on Wednesday. Will that work for you?"

Five Star Service Scheduling allows you to start your first patient on time, complete on time, and still have a quality conversation with your patients. Being unrushed and on time is one of the best ways to spread your reputation of excellent and timely service.

Bill Blatchford, DDS

From the Blatchford Play Book: Practice Drills

The Davis-Matthews team practice in regularly scheduled BMW 4x4 skill building sessions.

➤ Create phone skills, tag line and message that set you apart. It is your first opportunity to impress. Be bold, be different

➤ Cross train each team member including the Doctor. Learn to answer the phone, make firm financial arrangements, having meaningful conversations about patient dreams, clean a room, run a day sheet, sharpen instruments, make appointments and operate the computer.

➤ Practice introducing guests to staff members, sharing what you have learned and make your guest feel special.

➤ Analyze some plays that have not worked in your office. Make changes, build skills and reconstruct confidence to move forward

➤ Join Toastmaster's to learn confidence

➤ Always practice harder than you expect to play

➤ Video tape your role play sessions

➤ Analyze your video tapes

➤ Study what worked and duplicate that behavior

➤ Create plans for every situation, follow the plan

23

THE GIFT OF GIVING

Drs. Jayson Tabor

Dr. Tabor of Hendersonville, TN is a well-rounded dentist with wife, Mary Beth, who has a general dentistry practice which focuses on children. Together are raising four little girls. His wife would say, before Blatchford, he was consumed by his practice, had lots of stress and very few vacations, with the exception of mission trips. Today, Jayson is multifaceted, less stressed, a better father, because the Blatchford coaching allowed him to be true to the person he really was. The real Jayson is present.

Jayson confirms fear can consume you. One can have fear to take time off as it seems like everything will fall apart if you do not appear on a regular basis. Once you can conquer your false fears, for Jayson, home becomes home and work becomes work. The two do not mix and that equals less stress.

They take seven weeks off and other non-Blatchford dentists laugh at having a team with all that time off. Jayson really gets the Blatchford concept of productive, vacation, productive, vacation. Dentistry, by nature, can be stressful and that makes the vacation phase or the opportunity to recoup that much more critical. Doctor and team need time away to avoid burnout and are thus ultimately more productive and provide better dentistry for their patients. Jayson says it really works.

Jayson actually purchased his dad's dental practice a few years out of dental school. He is the only dental sibling so a regular sale transpired with his dad financing it as his dad continued to work two days a week for seven years. During this time, Jayson took Invisalign, Misch's Implant course, Kois Center education, short-term orthodontics and DOCS. His father became certified in IV Sedation, which Jayson did later.

Jayson has had a 25% increase in production since beginning with Blatchford Coaching about two years ago and has achieved that with one less team member than when he started. He feels the financial gain is not the most important benefit of Blatchford for him. He is more fulfilled with having better, more quality time with his family when he is not at work. This results in a better work-life balance. Jayson feels when you live with no margin in your work-life balance, stress becomes king and can negatively impact the course of one's life. But if you flip that and take control of the work-life balance then the joy of life comes easily and naturally and everything is impacted positively. Improper work-life balance creates stress, which causes us to operate from a position of scarcity. Proper work-life balance causes us to operate from a position of abundance, which leads to greater gratitude and fullness of every aspect of life.

Jayson's wife, Mary Beth, a dental school classmate, is a general dentist who only sees children in the same building. Her practice is actually in the space which previously was Jayson's father's private office. It has three pedo bench chairs and she runs an efficient practice. Jayson jokingly says, "Mary Beth was Blatchford before they were even into Blatchford." Spouses working together has challenges but now it's better than ever and they are so grateful.

One of the passions Jayson and Mary Beth have is serving through international medical and dental missions. Their Christian belief is God has given them a calling to serve others with their skill. When

Jayson and Mary Beth were in dental school, they participated in a dental mission trip to El Salvador. They knew then, God had called them to this and that they would continue to serve others in developing countries with their trade as long as they were able. Jayson feels there is a spiritual connection when serving other in the mission field. He says that since we are all God's children, it is important that we live and treat others accordingly. Jayson's father has been on several of these trips with him, along with volunteering in the forensic dentistry effort in NYC following 9/11.

Jayson is leading a dental volunteer group to Haiti for an exhilarating week twice a year. Extracting as many as 100 teeth daily in high-90 degree temperatures is all worth it when we think about how we can impact the life of some people in extremely desperate life circumstances. Currently there is great momentum with their group, Hope Smiles, in Haiti. Their goal is to partner with the Haitian dental community to train, lead and equip them to be better in their profession and provide a higher level of care for their fellow Haitian. Since most Haitian dental students leave the country or abandon the profession early, this will be a highly valuable asset to the people of Haiti. Jayson says they are trying to teach them to fish, not just handout fish, when they go down there. This takes the whole short-term mission trip to another level because it is creating a sustainable environment for this mission to continue for a long time. He is leading a team of Blatchford Doctors in September of 2017, including Bill and Christina.

Along with volunteering "away" from home, Jayson has helped establish a dental clinic in Hendersonville serving the working uninsured, called the Salvus Dental Clinic. Initially, there were three dentists volunteering rotating through the Fridays-only clinic. Jayson and others raised funds and equipment for a real physical location that is housed in the basement of their Sumner County Health Department. Well equipped, there are now more than 30 dentists who volunteer at the clinic.

Jayson as a leader of his dental team has a connection that is much deeper and more effective. He feels stress is a disease and to relieve stress, it affects everything. His team is bonusing about $1000 each for the BAM period. They own their jobs and the results. They have skin in the game and they work harder.

Dr. Tabor had previously been through a couple of different practice management services, unsuccessfully. He was so stressed at work, he knew he had to do something. He called around to different ones and felt that Blatchford was the only one who was training their dentists to be better leaders and to be better equipped for the future.

www.smilesthatrock.com

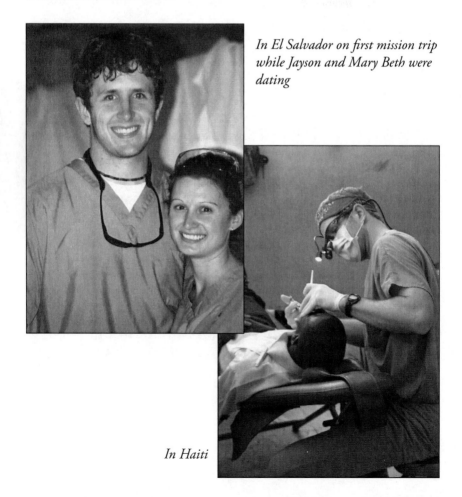

In El Salvador on first mission trip while Jayson and Mary Beth were dating

In Haiti

In Haiti

The Tabor family

Blatchford Game Plan: Rightsize for Profitability

Many dentists feel they walk a tightrope between caring for all the patients who seek better dental health vs. having meaningful, productive days. They feel there is a balancing act between having adequate and fully trained staff and profitability. How can a dentist diagnose ideal dentistry and not become a financial institution for many patients?

Staffing a practice with committed partners, operating at 55% overhead, providing care for quality "A" patients who see the value of treatment you have to offer and feeling satisfaction or even delight at the end of the day for a job well done—can actually occur. A dentist can have a profitable practice and perform ideal dentistry with a plan to reach those goals.

When a dentist and staff do not fully understand the economics of a small business, a roller-coaster effect results with vast differences in monthly production and collections. Dental practices are many times staffed, equipped and supplied for producing between 50% and 100% more than is actually produced. This results in a practice constantly chasing their overhead which creates stress emotionally, physically and in the checkbook.

Why not staff for the present production, gather and serve "A" patients who see value in your excellent dentistry and all can be produced at 55% overhead, leaving a net of 45% every month. What is the plan? It is called "rightsizing."

Rightsizing a practice reduces overhead immediately to produce a profit whatever size you are now. How can some doctors net $250,000 out of $600,000 gross production and other doctors must produce $800,000 to $1,000,000 to net $200,000? The smaller practice is "rightsized." A larger practice with multiple doctors is not always the most profitable. In fact, the profitability is more difficult to control as "bigness' creates layers of management which is not necessary in a smaller practice.

Many dentists operate their practices on hope. They are staffed to produce and collect what they hope. Many dental practices are actually staffed for double what they really produce and collect.

Rightsizing is operating a practice where the numbers work well no matter the outside economic factors or what the newspapers are shouting. A rightsized practice is profitable at whatever size. We work with doctors who have one staff member and their net return is 50%. We have practices with several doctors and their net return is 45%.

Rightsizing your practice is having the statistics work well for your practice now and laying concrete groundwork and goals for where you are headed in the future. Rightsizing your practice occurs when the leader of the practice takes a hard look at where he is headed, makes some assessments and clearly shifts to the direction for which he wants to be remembered.

What would be some benefits of a more controlled practice?

- An immediate increase in net income.
- By utilizing Block Scheduling, you perform more quality work on fewer numbers of patients, thus requiring a smaller staff.
- You determine the pace rather than being "Everything to Everybody."
- Team is easier to manage and direct with committed and highly skilled players.
- Overhead is reduced and productivity increases when number of staff is smaller.
- Team communication is greater with fewer, more focused staff.
- Dental office becomes as stressless as possible with the doctor seeing no more than 14 patients a day.
- Patients perceive quality care, quality time and quality staff.
- They refer patients with similar values.

More, bigger, bigger is no longer the desirable practice model for dentistry. It is difficult to have a favorable economic return with seven chairs, ten staff members and the doctor seeing 25 to 30 patients a day. A typical overhead in that office would be 80%. And the dentist and his staff worked hard! Yet, patients perceive this office as a dental factory with the doctor making rounds on his jet-powered roller skates and the "girls doing all the work."

Instead of management out of control with too many underpaid staff members and an exhausted frustrated dentist, let's practice with a model which has the right balance for ease, quality treatment and net return for the doctor.

What is wanted and needed in dentistry is an efficient practice that can serve patients expediently. A smaller, efficient practice can be very rewarding and work well. It does require several important criteria to produce the results you want:

LEADERSHIP: The dentist needs to have a clear focus or picture of the standard of care he wants to deliver, the quality of patients he wants and the contribution he wants to leave in the community. He must be excited about the dentistry and patients he serves. His motivation and delight must show.

TEAM: When the dentist has a clear picture of where he wants to go in dentistry, staff members who want to make the same contribution will be drawn to the practice. In hiring quality staff, the attitude and the people skills weigh more heavily than the technical skills, which can be learned by a motivated person.

SYSTEMS: Business and technical systems must be in place (see checklist).

CASE PRESENTATION: The dentist and staff must become very skilled in the area of case presentation, acceptance and financial arrangements. This requires asking the patient questions and listening, rather than you speaking. Case presentation is a learned skill that must be practiced continually. You are presenting to patients the possibility of keeping their teeth for a lifetime.

BLOCK SCHEDULING: Implement a daily template of how you want your day to be with 80% of the productive work completed by lunch. Hold blocks of time open in the mornings for major procedures. Schedule towards a goal. Your patients receive undivided attention, you are "on time" and they perceive your impeccable asepsis techniques.

An argument could be made that the dentist could not possibly change the size and format of his practice because he needs all his staff to perform the work. This is true. You do need all the present staff if you continue to practice the same way when seeing 25 to 30 patients a day.

Rightsizing is an opportunity to look at the possibility of attracting and keeping "A" patients who appreciate you timeliness, quality and service. Analyze the "B" and "C" patients you continue to treat to have them show up as "A's" in your practice or encourage them to find care where they might show up as an "A" in the other practice.

Doctors might say, "Rightsizing sounds good but I just don't have the quantity of quality patients to fill the morning blocks with permanent work." Virtually every practice has a large number of "A" patients who are very loyal to you. What has been missing is a clear direction from the leader as to the standard of care for which he/she wants to be remembered.

Once that standard is established, the team needs skill building in the area of case presentation. Ask questions of your existing "A" patients which will have them visualize the kind of smile they would really like.

Present to your existing patients the opportunity for lifetime dental plans. Set goals with them for permanent quality dentistry. It may be accomplished a phase at a time and it will be appreciated.

The advantages of rightsizing your practice are many.

- With staff overhead at 20%, profitability returns for doctor and staff with a bonus plan.

- By focusing on quality more permanent work, the practice attracts patients who want that work and refer their family and friends.

- With fewer team members, each is accountable for the result. Team members learn to work more efficiently.

- The dentist has the opportunity to focus the practice in the direction of choice rather than treating everyone.

- With block booking in place, patients receive the undivided attention of the professional team. No other patients are seen during those reserved blocks. Patients receive extraordinary service by unhurried professionals.

- By rightsizing your practice, you are attracting those patients who want the same type of dentistry being delivered. The team can be well-compensated and patients will be receiving the attention and service they want and deserve.

CHECK LIST FOR RIGHTSIZING

Leadership:

1. Doctor has defined picture of practice in ten years, 20 years and has shared that with staff.

2. Doctor has set standard of care for his practice.

3. Doctor knows and shares the numbers in the practice.

4. Doctor is excited about dentistry and his patients.

5. Doctor is able to let go and delegate tasks.

Team:

1. Committed team players for staff.

2. Morning meetings to set the day.

3. Weekly team meetings which produce results.

4. Team participates in a bonus plan.

Systems:

1. Block scheduling in place for doctor and hygiene.

2. Office financial policy in place with agreement that no treatment is scheduled without financial arrangements.

3. Financial choices available to patient include outside funding sources.

4. Over the counter collection goal is 35% of production.

5. Establish a short call list, insurance profile notebook and pending treatment book.

Case Presentation:

1. Gather a library of books, audios and videos on sales and staff skill-building with team.

2. Ask the patient "open ended" questions (which cannot be answered with "yes" or "no".)

3. Avoid giving the Dentistry 101 lecture with pictures on each phase of treatment.

4. Include instamatic pictures of patient for your record taking. Patients get to see their own teeth and smiles.

5. Use before and after pictures to create interest with patients.

6. Present life-time treatment plans to all patients.

Bill Blatchford, DDS

From the Blatchford Play Book:
Turning Your Weakness Into a Strength

As Drs. Tabor can testify, dentists can and need to have their house in order to flourish, no matter the cause. Systems and skills need to be practiced and mastered. Strengthening your life priorities and evaluating your strengths before you need them is essential to keep a balanced life and successful practice moving forward.

► Face your fears for they will keep you weak

► One permanent emotion of the inferior man is fear—fear of the unknown, the complex, the inexplicable. What he wants beyond everything is safety.

► Anyone can conquer fear by doing things he fears to do, providing he keeps doing them until he gets a record of successful experiences behind him

► What are your weaknesses? Put yourself under a microscope.

► How good do you want to be?

► When the game is on the line, there is no substitute for skill

► Eliminate your negative qualities

► Do not let your weaknesses master you

► Do not use your weaknesses as an excuse

► Be willing to be uncomfortable

► Work on your weaknesses

► Always remember, behavior is a choice

► Chose positive and productive behavior

CONCLUSION

Over the last thirty years, I have coached over 2,800 dental offices for success. Each dentist's goals and aspirations determine their success. It is different for each person. Success is doing what you think is rewarding. The rewards are also as individual as the definition of success. Our society tends to measure success by material measurements yet, these stories of real people demonstrate each has their own measure. We selected stories from all parts of the country and various levels of income. Each story is unique and all are successful in their own way. Each has shared their personal story about their professional life and practice. They speak of what worked and shared pitfalls as well. They have shared what motivates them and their frustrations. Each is different. All have been our clients, some on a continuing regular basis and others we have not had regular contact for some time. It is rewarding for me to see that we made an impact on their lives and practices. We enjoy seeing that they have kept on "keeping on" with the direction they set while working with Blatchford Solutions.

After observing many dentists in their offices, we have found several common characteristics which contribute to success. These are shared in all the stories and more importantly, by all success practices. We have always studied why some dentist are successful and make it look easy while others struggle and are constantly dissatisfied. We have found that behind all of those who make it look easy, there has been a lot of hard work and dedication. A wise man once said, "Successful people make a habit of doing those things that others know about and choose not to do." **There are no secrets**. Knowledge is valuable yet many do not put it into action. Many dentists are very academic and study every situation until the opportunity goes away. It is also called "paralysis by analysis."

The first and most important trait we have observed in a successful dentist is a strong sense of **purpose or vision**. This is known but few actually practice it. A study of *Man's Search for Meaning* by Victor Frankel illustrates how vision is a compelling force. Vision offers the bigger picture. It is the motivating force that gets one through hard times. One must have a bigger picture of life and what you want to accomplish in your short stay on the planet. People with vision have a positive outlook on life and exhibit this daily. For them, failures are just opportunities to learn. They have failures but get over them quickly and move on with their life. For them, the glass is either full or half full. For them it is never empty or half empty. As Helen Keller said, "Life is either a daring adventure or nothing at all." Vision is what drives these people to always trying to improve. We observe each of these dentists has a living a vision many believe not possible. All believe if it has been done, it must be possible. They even believe if it has not been done, it may be possible.

The next common characteristic is clear **goals** which are much more concrete than vision statements. Many people go through life without any goals. They seldom accomplish much and are constantly dissatisfied. All of these doctors have very clear goals. They gain satisfaction by accomplishing a goal and moving to the next one. If they do not reach a goal, they keep trying. We believe that the happiest dentists are the ones who have goals in all areas of their life and have balance as a result of this. Goals must be specific. Can you measure it? Goals that are not specific are not really goals but just passing thoughts. Nonspecific goals are also known as wishes. Goals must have a time line. A "by when" this will be complete. It is too easy to put off making things happen.

There must be some form of affirmation. You must write them down and review constantly. Share them only with someone committed to your success. Do not share them with the naysayers for they will try to discourage you. Most people without goals (95% of the population) do not share your enthusiasm for life and success. All of these stories share goals and how they were accomplished. They have also shared setbacks along the way.

All of these dentists share the third characteristic of **constant learning**; continually learning new techniques. They are reading and taking courses. They are willing to spend the time and money to seek the best teachers in our profession. They are not satisfied with the minimum. They take the comprehensive courses to master a topic; not satisfied with only a short course. Besides learning new techniques, they have learned you do not have to spend time trying to reinvent the wheel. The wheel is already invented and if it worked for someone it may work for them also. They are constantly striving to be the best. They are open-minded and are very willing to look at different ways to accomplish things. They are constantly reminded of Dr. Omer Reed's quote, "You do not know what you do not know." As soon as we think we know something, we stop asking questions. When we stop asking questions, we stop learning. When we stop learning, we die spiritually.

The fifth characteristic we see in all of these stories is **surrounding yourself with great people**. It is not just mentors but also having a great team. There are several common rules for attracting and keeping great team members. One is the doctor's clear vision and what will it take to get there. You must decide what the position entails and then hire to the position, not adapt the position to fit the person. Set high standards and lead by example. Always hire for attitude. You can train someone with a great attitude to do anything but you cannot teach anything to someone with a poor attitude. Attitude is manifested as behavior and behavior is always a choice. Hire people with great behavior. Several of these stories indicate how they kept people with poor attitude too long.

They have all set up systems of accountability. All of the dentists have learned the value of rewarding the team well. All want their team to be the best paid in town. They constantly look for areas to compliment their team. There must be accountability in each area for their team to flourish. The successful doctors in this book are quick to acknowledge great performance. While it is fine to like your team members, you must remain the leader. You did not hire them to be a pal. There is a reason that in the military officers are prohibited from fraternizing with the enlisted personnel.

The sixth characteristic is an **awareness of the business** of dentistry. While they are not micro managers, they study the numbers and own them. They have discovered what numbers are important. They know their cost per hour. What does it cost to do a unit of Crown and Bridge? What does it cost to see a hygiene patient? What does it cost when a patient cancels or no shows? What procedures actually make money for the practice? They realize that by doubling hygiene production per day, it is less than one additional unit of C&B. they realize what a fee increase does for the bottom line. They know if they keep their staff overhead between 15-20% of their gross, the numbers fall into line. They know it is better to pay individuals well, but not have as many total staff. They understand they want their lab to be over 10% of their gross. If it is lower, they are not effective in showing value to their guests. They know their diagnosis to appointment ratio. What is their new patient per month flow? Where do these patients come from? They recognize the value of a marketing budget. These dentists do not receive their marketing advice from internet forums. They have a long-range plan by establishing a budget and either hiring professionals or studying the local market themselves. One characteristic of these doctors is awareness of the bigger picture and not worry what percentage they spend on the dental supplies or lab. They understand quality and are willing to charge a fair fee not dictated by insurance companies. Several of the doctors in the book charge fee plus lab or fee plus implant for discretionary items.

The seventh characteristic is the **willingness to be courageous in marketing**. All are doing some form of marketing. They recognize they are in a discretionary form of treatment and must let the public know what they do. All have a website and they rely on it for new patient flow. They use it to inform and educate. They promote the website every way they can. Social media is all important. Several are using radio on a regular basis. Several use print media. Some are using television. Several have filmed their own Extreme Makeover shows. All are doing some form of networking to let people know who they are and what they do. All of this has taken courage to break the mold from traditional attitudes about marketing. Several have grown by purchasing practices and merging with their existing patient base. In each case, they have had to establish a budget and act on faith. They are always looking for ways to promote their practice to the right people.

The eighth and last characteristic is the **development of superior communications skills**. They have learned how to first communicate with their team. By doing this, they do not have to micro-manage every detail. They are able to paint the big picture and stand back letting team members move forward. The doctors in the book realize team members have good ideas and allow them to be true team members. The leader's job is to create an environment for learning. They realize that the most important skill not only in their practice but in their life is communication. This is the ability to communicate their vision and to discover other people's vision. They realize they cannot be all things to all people.

These characteristics seem to run common throughout all the dentists in this book and are also common among all successful people. The main characteristic of all these people is the choice to do those things that unsuccessful people know about and choose not to do.

Christina Blatchford, DMD
Bill Blatchford, DDS

*Loyola dental student Bill Blatchford practicing denture setup
in his Chicago kitchen, 1967.*

Blatchford Custom Coaching

- Just starting a practice and want to do it right the first time?
- Are you working too hard and not being rewarded?
- Do you feel your leadership is less than stellar?
- Are you practicing the type of dentistry you enjoy or are you being restricted by insurance companies?

Blatchford's Custom Coaching allows doctors to reach their individual and practice goals. Not a cookie cutter approach, the goals achieved and resulting model occurs because Coaches Blatchford help doctors discover and clarify their own goals, values and dreams.

With 57 years combined experience in the dental field, Bill and Christina have a no-nonsense approach. Their goal is your goal.

Custom Coaching is 14 months of one-on-one coaching with our three dentist/coaches. A full-day summit with your dentist/coach and several others is filled with personal discovery, introspection, revelation and commitment.

Each client has a monthly individual coaching call with one of our dentist/coaches. A call prep sheet is submitted prior to the call to ensure the most pressing positives and concerns are addressed.

Two team seminars (two days each) are packed with energy, systems, team accountability and skill building. Separate monthly conference calls on timely topics are held for doctor and team members. A Blatchford professional consultant has regular contact and in-house learning.

Additional Resources

Most of the doctors featured in this book have given video testimonials. These are available at
www.blatchford.com/testimonials

Also please visit our YouTube Channel
www.youtube.com/morningswithblatchford
Mornings With Blatchford is Inspirational Practice Management Tips No One Else in Dentistry is Sharing

Phone Number to Schedule a Call with Dr. Bill Blatchford or Dr. Christina Blatchford
888-495-7080

Email Drs. Blatchford
info@blatchford.com

Blatchford Solutions Official Website
www.blatchford.com

Video Testimonials from Blatchford Solutions Clients
www.blatchford.com/testimonials

Blatchford Solutions Facebook Page
www.facebook.com/blatchfordsolutions

Webinar: 7 Simple Systems to Attract New Patients With Money
www.blatchford.com/webinar

Webinar: 22 Systems for Maximum Profitability and More Time Off
www.blatchford.com/systems

Report: What the Top Women Dentists Are Doing That You Are Not
www.blatchford.com/women

Report: 7 Mistakes Most Dentists Make When Buying or Selling a Practice or Adding An Associate
www.blatchford.com/7mistakes

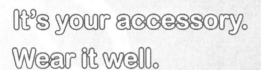

It's your accessory.
Wear it well.

Fabulous accessories are a girl's way of saying "this is who I am," without saying a word. A perfect smile by Dr. Okamura and team is a timeless accessory that will scream "*This is me!*" across any room, every day for the rest of your life. Yes, even louder than your rhinestone glasses, though they *are* fabulous.

KIM OKAMURA, DDS
DESIGNING BEAUTIFUL SMILES

BriteSmile® • Invisalign® • Veneers • Natural-looking Restorations • General Dentistry

11730 15th Avenue NE   Seattle   Washington   98125   206.362.3200   www.kimokamuradds.com